Who Killed
the American Dream?

Recent books by Thom Hartmann

The Hidden History of the American Dream: The Demise of the Middle Class—and How to Rescue Our Future

The Hidden History of American Democracy: Rediscovering Humanity's Ancient Way of Living

The Hidden History of Neoliberalism: How Reaganism Gutted America and How to Restore Its Greatness

The Hidden History of Big Brother in America: How the Death of Privacy and the Rise of Surveillance Threaten Us and Our Democracy

The Hidden History of American Healthcare: Why Sickness Bankrupts You and Makes Others Insanely Rich

The Hidden History of American Oligarchy: Reclaiming Our Democracy from the Ruling Class

The Hidden History of Monopolies: How Big Business Destroyed the American Dream

The Hidden History of the War on Voting: Who Stole Your Vote—and How to Get It Back

The Hidden History of the Supreme Court and the Betrayal of America

The Hidden History of Guns and the Second Amendment

Who Killed the American Dream?

The Greatest Political Crime Ever Told

THOM HARTMANN

Berrett-Koehler

PUBLISHERS

Berrett-Koehler Publishers, Inc.
1333 Broadway, Suite P100
Oakland, CA 94612-1921
(510) 817-2277
bkconnection.com

Ordering Information
Quantity sales. Special discounts are available on quantity purchases by corporations, associations, individuals, and others. For details, please go to bkconnection.com to see our bulk discounts or contact bookorders@bkpub.com for more information.
Textbook exam/desk copies. Please consult the General FAQ at bkconnection.com.
Bookstore orders for trade or textbook use. For print books, please contact Penguin Random House Publisher Services at customerservice@penguinrandomhouse.com. For ebooks, contact your favorite distributor.

Distributed to the US trade and internationally by Penguin Random House Publisher Services.

The authorized representative in the EU for product safety and compliance is EU Compliance Partner, Pärnu mnt. 139b-14, 11317 Tallinn, Estonia, www.eucompliancepartner.com, +372 5368 65 02.

Berrett-Koehler and the BK logo are registered trademarks of Berrett-Koehler Publishers, Inc.

Printed in the United States of America

Berrett-Koehler books are printed on long-lasting acid-free paper. When it is available, we choose paper that has been manufactured by environmentally responsible processes. These may include using trees grown in sustainable forests, incorporating recycled paper, minimizing chlorine in bleaching, or recycling the energy produced at the paper mill.

Cataloging-in-Publication Data is on file at the Library of Congress.
Names: Hartmann, Thom, 1951–   author
Title: Who killed the American dream? : the greatest political crime ever told / Thom Hartmann.
Description: First edition. | Oakland, CA : Berrett-Koehler Publishers, 2026. | Includes bibliographical references and index.
Identifiers: LCCN 2026008255 (print) | LCCN 2026008256 (ebook) | ISBN 9798890572639 paperback | ISBN 9798890572646 pdf | ISBN 9798890572653 epub
Subjects: LCSH: Corporations—Corrupt practices—United States | Corporation law—United States—Criminal provisions | Corporate power—United States | Juristic persons—United States | United States. Supreme Court—Decision making
Classification: LCC KF9351 .H37 2026 (print) | LCC KF9351 (ebook)
LC record available at https://lccn.loc.gov/2026008255
LC ebook record available at https://lccn.loc.gov/2026008256

First Edition

35 34 33 32 31 30 29 28 27 26   †   10 9 8 7 6 5 4 3 2 1

Book production: BookMatters
Cover design: Ashley Ingram
Cover illustration: Generated by Nano Banana AI

Contents

Author's Note

For over a century, independent researchers and the occasional individual have made the same discovery I did: that the Supreme Court never granted corporations the rights that they are claiming today. The best have been Howard Jay Graham,[1] Jeffrey Clements,[2] and the people at Move to Amend.

Some have written about it, spoken about it, or even written books about it, but the message never seems to have broken through to the general public. It's my hope that by writing my story, this will wake up enough Americans to lead to positive change back in the direction of democracy in our republic.

Who Killed
the American Dream?

A Crime in Plain Sight

Every law student in America learns the same story: "In 1886, the United States Supreme Court ruled in *Santa Clara County v. Southern Pacific Railroad Company* that corporations are persons under the Fourteenth Amendment. This single decision fundamentally transformed American democracy, business, and law. It granted corporations the same constitutional rights as human beings: free speech, due process, equal protection. Everything that followed, from unlimited corporate campaign spending to corporate control of our media, politics, and environment, traces back to that pivotal moment."

There's just one problem: It never happened. The Supreme Court debated this issue and never made that ruling. Not in 1886, not ever.

What actually happened is far more disturbing: A court reporter, a corrupt Supreme Court justice, and the railroad oligarchs who owned America's most powerful corporations successfully conspired to rewrite the Constitution. They committed the crime in broad daylight, recorded it in official court documents, and hid it in plain sight for 140 years.

This is both a detective story and a true crime investigation. Like all good mysteries, it starts with a discovery, mine, in a dusty Vermont law library on a cold winter day in 2002.

The Library Discovery

I thought I was confirming a fact. Instead, I uncovered a crime scene.

I was researching corporate power in America, working in the Vermont Supreme Court library six blocks from my then-home in Montpelier.

Every legal textbook, every encyclopedia, every Supreme Court case for the past hundred-plus years cited the same precedent: *Santa Clara County v. Southern Pacific Railroad Company* (1886) established that corporations are persons under the Fourteenth Amendment.

The reason I was in the library was simple: I wanted to read the actual decision, not summaries, not commentary, but the words the Supreme Court actually wrote.

The Vermont Supreme Court library contains one of the most comprehensive collections of legal documents in New England. Librarian Paul Donovan pulled down Volume 118 of *United States Reports*: Cases Adjudged in the Supreme Court at October Term 1885 and October Term 1886. The book was published in 1888 by Banks & Brothers in New York, written by J.C. Bancroft Davis, the Supreme Court's official reporter.

The volume was heavy in my hands, its leather binding cracked with age, pages giving off that distinctive smell of vanilla and dust that old books possess, the scent of history itself.

I found the case—page 394. What I discovered there would change everything I thought I knew about American democracy.

The decision itself, the actual legal ruling written by Justice Harlan, said nothing about corporate constitutional rights. In fact, it explicitly stated that the Court was not deciding that constitutional question. The Court instead ruled on a narrow technical issue about fence-post assessments and California property tax law. Corporate constitutional rights under the Fourteenth Amendment were not addressed, not decided, and not even meaningfully mentioned.

But at the top of the case, before the decision itself, sat something called a "headnote" which said, in part: "The defendant Corporations are persons within the intent of the clause in section 1 of the Fourteenth Amendment to the Constitution of the United States, which forbids a State to deny to any person within its jurisdiction the equal protection of the laws."

I read it again. Then again. My coffee grew cold on the table beside me.

The headnote claimed that under the Constitution corporations were persons.

The decision explicitly refused to rule on that question.

One of them was lying.

I paid seventy cents for photocopies and walked through the crisp winter air to the office of Jim Ritvo, a local attorney and friend.

"What's a headnote?" I asked, spreading the pages on his desk.

He leaned back in his chair, studying the documents. "Court reporters write them. They're summaries for lawyers, convenient shortcuts to understand what a case is about without reading the whole thing." He looked up at me. "But Thom, headnotes aren't law. They're not part of the decision. They have no legal standing whatsoever."

"So, this headnote that says corporations are persons…"

"Isn't law," he finished. "Never was."

I felt the floor shift beneath me.

"But every case since 1886 cites this as precedent! Law schools teach it. The Supreme Court itself cited it more than a dozen times."

Jim picked up the pages, reading more carefully. "Then somebody's been fooled for a very long time. Or somebody's been doing the fooling."

The American Dream Is Murdered

I didn't know it yet, standing in that Vermont library, but I was about to discover why my generation was the last to experience the American Dream as our parents and grandparents knew it.

When my Boomer generation was the same average age as Millennials are today, back in 1990, we held 21.3 percent of the nation's wealth. Louise and I shared in that wealth: although we were still in our 30s, in 1990 we owned a profitable small business—our fourth—and a nice home.

Our own locally owned business, a home of our own, and the knowledge that our kids would have more opportunities than we did: that was, in fact, one common way of defining the American Dream. It was normal then.

My dad, born in 1928, worked in a tool and die shop. He was able to buy a house, a new car every two years, and take a two-week vacation every year because the middle class in America before the Reagan Revolution had a pretty damn good life. Dad retired in the 1990s with a full pension that let him and my mom travel the world. He lived the American Dream, as did his four boys.

Millennials today, by contrast, are roughly the same number of people as Boomers were in 1990 but hold only 4.6 percent of the nation's wealth. If they're the same age I was in 1990, they're most likely struggling to own a home, are deeply in debt, and find it nearly impossible to start a small business.

This is what a bizarre theory called "corporate personhood" or "corporate constitutional rights" has brought us to. Boomers in their 30s owned 21.3 percent of the nation's wealth, while Millennials in their 30s today own a mere 4.6 percent of the nation's wealth.

And the story for Zoomers, those born in the late 1990s and early 2000s, is pretty much the same, if not slightly worse.

What happened?

The answer was there on page 394 of that musty law book. A single fraudulent sentence that gave America's oligarchs and the corporations that made them rich the constitutional weapons to dismantle everything that made America work for working people.

Why did my children's generation face stagnant wages while across the nation worker productivity soared? Why did crushing student debt replace the free or near-free college my generation enjoyed? Why did housing costs explode from two times annual income to ten times annual income? Why did healthcare go from a manageable expense to the leading cause of bankruptcy in America? Why did the promise that hard work would be rewarded with security become a cruel joke for tens of millions of Americans?

Virtually all of it came about because of corporate constitutional rights.

That fraudulent headnote gave corporations constitutional rights they could wield against democratic governance. Against unions. Against environmental protections. Against consumer safety laws. Against taxes that funded public goods. Against anything and everything that built and sustained the American middle class.

The American Dream didn't just fade away: it was murdered. And the murder weapon was forged in 1886 and then lifted against all of us with the 1980s Reagan Revolution.

The Investigation Begins

I spent the next few weeks in that library, pulling case after case. The pattern was unmistakable. Dozens, then hundreds, then thousands of court decisions cited *Santa Clara* as establishing corporate constitutional rights. They cited it the same way, always referencing that headnote but never quoting the decision itself that contradicted it.

The legal profession had been fooled. Or perhaps more accurately, it had fooled itself, generation after generation of lawyers and judges accepting what they'd been taught without checking the original source.

But who wrote that headnote? And why? Is this what they intended? And what does it mean not just for working-class people but for our democracy itself?

The answer to those questions would lead me deep into one of the most consequential conspiracies in American history, a conspiracy involving railroad oligarchs who controlled more wealth than entire nations, a Supreme Court justice whose corruption was hiding in plain sight, and a court reporter whose single fraudulent sentence would reshape American democracy for more than a century.

This book tells that story. But it tells more than that.

It reveals how that original crime in 1886 metastasized into today's corporate domination of our economy, our media, our politics, and our lives. How the oligarchs of this era—the billionaires who control corporations like ExxonMobil, Amazon, Goldman Sachs, Google, and Comcast—are the direct heirs to those railroad barons. How they've used the same legal fiction to accumulate unprecedented power and transfer over fifty trillion dollars from working Americans to their own money bins just over the past four decades.

It shows how two Progressive Eras, from the 1890s through 1921 and again from 1933 through 1981, built the American Dream by constraining corporate power. How the Founders understood the dangers of corporate tyranny and deliberately excluded corporations from constitutional protection. How FDR's recognition that "necessitous men are not free men" led to the creation of the largest middle class in world history, with two-thirds of Americans achieving middle-class status by the day Reagan was sworn in as president on January 20, 1981.

And it shows how corporate constitutional rights gave America's oligarchs, Ronald Reagan, George W. Bush, and Donald Trump, the weapons they needed to tear it all down. To crush unions. To slash taxes on the wealthy. To offshore our factories. To turn healthcare into a profit center. To transform housing into a speculative commodity. To burden our children with crushing debt for the education that was once free or nearly free.[3]

All to make themselves richer than any king, emperor, or pharaoh in all of human history.

The Cover-Up and the Solutions

But stealing our constitutional rights wasn't enough; to get away with the crime, the perpetrators needed to hide it. They needed to make sure that when working Americans asked, "Who killed the American Dream?" they'd blame the wrong people.

Thus, they began a cover-up of the crime, in part, as an effort to slip it into subsequent Supreme Court decisions to make it law and, in part, as an effort to disguise the crime itself from current and future generations.

Over the past fifty or so years, the most effective part of the deflection—or cover-up playbook—has been a remarkably successful effort to divert Americans' attention and anger away from the oligarchs and corporations that are actively undermining our democracy and get people to instead blame their woes on women, people of color, welfare recipients, and, most recently, nonwhite immigrants.

Entire media operations have joined this effort, as I'll document in subsequent chapters. And it's been largely successful; most Americans—and certainly the Republican base—have bought the cover-up hook, line, and sinker. They have no idea that the same billionaires who own the media that keeps them fooled are also working hard to keep them down, and instead cheer every effort to "own the libs" rather than constraining corporate or billionaire power.

What You Can Do to Fight Back

Most importantly, this book shows how we can undo the crime. How we can restore democracy. How we can reclaim the rights that were stolen from us and given to artificial entities that exist only on paper. I'll detail for you exactly how we can rebuild the American Dream for our children and grandchildren.

There are multiple steps to reversing the abuse of human rights that this crime, committed in 1886, handed to corporations and America's oligarchs.

They include passing legislation to blunt some of the worst impacts (particularly on our politics, now that corporations and billionaires can legally buy elections), passing a constitutional amendment to prevent Republicans on the Supreme Court from continuing or expanding these "corporate constitutional rights," and waking up as many Americans as possible to this crime and its consequences.

We can fight back at every level of government (and you'll learn that people have been doing just this for decades with increasing success). Taking on this battle can be one of the most effective ways of re-empowering our democracy.

The rebellion has already begun; by the time you finish this book, you'll know how to join it.

But first, we need to understand exactly how the crime was committed.

1

The Scene of the Crime

THE CRIME TOOK PLACE IN WASHINGTON, DC, BUT ITS SEEDS WERE planted in California, where the most powerful corporation in America was waging war against democracy itself.

The Dawn of the First Progressive Era

To truly grasp the scope of the crime of 1886, you first have to understand what America was becoming at the time, and what the oligarchs were desperately trying to stop.

The 1880s started what historians would later call the First Progressive Era. After decades of unfettered corporate power following the Civil War, leading to brutal practices against workers, Americans were finally waking up and organizing. This rise of the new power of labor and communities demanding progressive changes had that era's oligarchs terrified.

By 1886, the Knights of Labor had grown to seven hundred thousand members, which made it the largest labor organization in American history. Workers, who'd been treated as disposable, were discovering their collective power and demanding an eight-hour workday, safer working conditions, and an actual living wage so they could support their families with dignity.

States were also beginning to regulate corporations in serious ways. These included new laws that limited working hours, required basic safety standards in factories and mines, and taxed corporate property to fund public schools, roads, mass transit, and other infrastructure that would benefit ordinary citizens beyond just the morbidly rich.

Farmers were organizing into state-based cooperatives, pooling their resources to escape the stranglehold of the railroad shipping monopolies and grain elevator cartels. The Grange movement had already won major victories in several states, confirming the newly recognized principle that state governments had the power to regulate corporations by citing the "public interest."

In short, the seeds of the American Dream—the promise that hard work would be rewarded with security and dignity, that ordinary people could own their own homes and businesses, that children would have opportunities their parents never had—were just beginning to sprout. The Progressive Era that would transform America and create the world's first widespread middle class was dawning.

The oligarchs and "conservative" politicians of that day well understood what was at stake. If this movement succeeded, if workers gained real power, if states could effectively regulate corporate activities, if taxes on the wealthy funded public goods that lifted all boats, then the era of rampant, unchecked corporate dominance would end. The railroad barons, the steel magnates, and the banking titans (among others) who'd accumulated unprecedented fortunes would have to share that power with America's democratic majority.

The oligarchs thus needed a weapon to fight back. They searched for years and finally found it in the Fourteenth Amendment, written to protect freed slaves but now soon to be perverted to protect corporate profits and oligarchic wealth.

The Railroad Oligarchs

In the 1880s, the Southern Pacific Railroad wasn't just a company: it essentially functioned as if it were a government unto itself.

The railroad controlled California's politics completely. Its executives owned senators, judges, governors, and newspaper editors. It had its own police force, its own courts and jails, and its own laws. When the railroad wanted something, the railroad got it. When it didn't want something, that thing didn't happen.

The men who owned the Southern Pacific—Leland Stanford, Collis

Huntington, Mark Hopkins, and Charles Crocker, known as the "Big Four"—were America's first oligarchs (other than the Southern plantation owners who'd tried to overthrow democracy and were defeated in the Civil War). They weren't just rich; they wielded their wealth as a weapon to bend local, state, and even the federal government to their collective will.

Stanford would later found Stanford University, laundering his reputation through philanthropy, the way many oligarchs have done ever since. But that came later; in the 1880s he was a railroad baron who saw democracy as an infuriating obstacle to ever-increasing profits and a challenge to his own personal wealth and political power.

And his railroad had a problem. California counties, under pressure from voters, were passing legislation that taxed railroad property to pay for public improvements including schools, roads, and bridges. The railroad barons, incensed, called this theft. They'd built their empires via federal land grants (Lincoln gave them tens of millions of acres during the Civil War), political corruption, and absolutely ruthless business practices. The idea that local communities could tax them to fund the common good seemed, to these railroad oligarchs, like an outrageous violation of their rights.

Most importantly, those taxes weren't just about revenue; they were also about power. They were about democratic communities saying out loud that they could control the corporations that operated in their territory. They claimed that corporations existed to serve public purposes, not the other way around.

If California could tax the railroads to fund public schools, the oligarchs reasoned, then children of workers might get educated. Educated workers would know how to demand better wages. Better wages would cut into railroad profits. If these affronts were allowed to stand, the whole system that kept the oligarchs on top might start to unravel.

So, Stanford and his buddies decided to manufacture a constitutional right that didn't exist: the right of corporations to be treated as "persons" under the Fourteenth Amendment. It was a preemptive strike against the Progressive Era before it had even fully emerged.

The Amendment Written in Blood

The Fourteenth Amendment was ratified in 1868, just three years after the Civil War ended. Its purpose was singular and clear: to guarantee that freed slaves would be recognized as full citizens with constitutional rights.

Section 1 contains the key language: "No State shall... deprive any person of life, liberty, or property, without due process of law; nor deny to any person within its jurisdiction the equal protection of the laws."

Over six hundred thousand Americans died in the Civil War; the Fourteenth Amendment was drafted in their blood. It was meant to ensure that the Black Americans for whom the war was fought would be protected by the Constitution. It was meant to guarantee that the promise of America—that all men are created equal, that every American deserved a chance at what Jefferson called "life, liberty, and the pursuit of happiness"—would finally apply to *all* Americans, regardless of the color of their skin.

The amendment carried the potential for real power, and it had already begun to transform the nature of America through Reconstruction, so the railroad oligarchs decided to exploit and corrupt it for their own purposes.

They'd tried before. During the first two decades after the Civil War following its ratification, corporations brought case after case to court, arguing that they were "persons" entitled to Fourteenth Amendment protections and thus access to the Bill of Rights (the first ten amendments to the Constitution). They lost. Repeatedly.

For example, in 1877, in *Munn v. Illinois*, the Supreme Court explicitly rejected the idea that corporations had the same rights as natural persons. Chief Justice Morrison Waite wrote for the majority that corporations were subject to "regulation...for the public good." Although they had a limited form of what today we'd call artificial personhood so they could sign contracts and pay taxes, they were not protected as if they were human persons under the Fourteenth Amendment.[4]

That decision was a victory for democracy. It affirmed what the Founders understood: that corporations are creations of law, subject to democratic control, not autonomous entities with the same "inherent rights" recognized for humans in the Bill of Rights. It meant that each of the states could regulate businesses in its own way, tax them fairly, and require them to serve the public interest.

If *Munn v. Illinois* had remained the law of the land, the reforms of the Progressive Era that followed might have been easier to achieve and harder to reverse. The American Dream might have taken root even earlier, and today we'd probably be far ahead even of Europe's most progressive democracies like Norway and Denmark, since we would have had such a huge head-start.

That failing, the oligarchs needed a new strategy.

The Tax Case

In 1882, the Southern Pacific Railroad simply stopped paying property taxes in several California counties, claiming the taxes were illegitimate. The counties sued, and the railroad fought back with an entirely new legal argument.

They claimed that those California counties' tax assessment methods violated the Fourteenth Amendment because they treated railroad property differently from other property, and that different counties had different tax rates. This "unequal protection," they argued, violated their rights as "persons" under the Constitution.

The case was *Santa Clara County v. Southern Pacific Railroad Company*. It worked its way through the lower courts for four years and finally reached the Supreme Court for the 1885/1886 term.

The railroad had advantages that most litigants lack. They had unlimited money for legal fees, political connections to judges and politicians, and, most importantly, they had something else: a friend on the Supreme Court itself.

US Supreme Court Associate Justice Stephen J. Field was a Californian who'd made his fortune during the Gold Rush. He owned railroad stock, socialized with railroad oligarchs, and believed, passionately, that corporations deserved constitutional protection from democratic governance.

Field's vision could be described as feudal. Like Edmund Burke generations earlier, he believed a small class of property owners should rule America, protected by the Constitution from the whims of the democratic majority. Wealth, he believed, was proof of goodness, wisdom, and competence, and poverty was a failure of the will.

The emerging middle class of the late mid-nineteenth century threatened this vision, in Field's view. Workers organizing into unions, farmers forming cooperatives, small businesses openly fighting the monopolies: all of this had to be stopped.

Field had been waiting for the right case, and *Santa Clara* would be it.

It started in 1883 because back then Supreme Court judges also "rode the circuit," working in their states as chief judges of the appeals courts most months of the year, and just spending a few months every year in Washington, DC, as justices of the Supreme Court.

So, in 1883, that case first came before Field in his capacity on the 9th Circuit Court of Appeals. He ruled in favor of the railroad, writing in his decision:

> The Fourteenth Amendment of the Constitution, in declaring that no State shall deny to any person within its jurisdiction the "equal protection of the laws," imposes a limitation upon the exercise of all the powers of the State which can touch the individual or his property, including that of taxation.
>
> The "equal protection of the laws" to any one implies not only that the means for the security of his private rights shall be accessible to him on the same terms with others, but also that he shall be exempt from any greater burdens or charges than such as are equally imposed upon all others under like circumstances. This equal protection forbids unequal exactions of any kind, and among them that of unequal taxation.[5]

Once Santa Clara County appealed their loss in the 9th Circuit, the case came before the US Supreme Court with Field himself as one of the men sitting in judgement.

The Oral Arguments

On January 26, 1886, the Supreme Court—with Justice Stephen J. Field in attendance—heard oral arguments in *Santa Clara County v.*

Southern Pacific Railroad Company.[6] J.C. Bancroft Davis, the Court's official reporter, took the notes, as did the county's lawyer, Delphin Delmas.

The railroad's lawyers made their pitch, echoing Field's decision in the 9th Circuit case: "The Fourteenth Amendment protects 'persons' from unequal treatment. Corporations are persons. Therefore, California's unequal tax assessment violates the railroad's constitutional rights."

The county's lawyers countered: "The Fourteenth Amendment was written to protect freed slaves who are actual humans, not railroad corporations. The framers never intended to grant constitutional rights to corporate artificial entities created by state law."

Then something weird happened.

Chief Justice Morrison Remick Waite interrupted the arguments. According to court records, he made an announcement: "The court does not wish to hear argument on the question whether the provision in the Fourteenth Amendment to the Constitution, which forbids a State to deny to any person within its jurisdiction the equal protection of the laws, applies to these corporations. We are all of the opinion that it does."[7]

The county's lawyer, trying to argue against the railroad's assertion that they were "persons" protected by the Fourteenth Amendment's Equal Protection Clause, was essentially told not to bother. The Court had already decided.

Or had it?

The Decision That Wasn't

On May 10, 1886, the Supreme Court laid down its decision in *Santa Clara County v. Southern Pacific Railroad Company.*

Justice John Marshall Harlan wrote the majority opinion. It's a technical, somewhat boring ruling about fence valuations and tax assessment procedures. The Court found in favor of the railroad, but not because of the Fourteenth Amendment; instead, it ruled that California had illegally included the value of the fences along the railroad right-of-way in the land's assessment in violation of its own laws.

Here's what Justice Harlan actually wrote in the *Santa Clara* opinion about corporate constitutional rights: *nothing.*

The Court's decision explicitly avoided the constitutional question. The Court instead ruled on narrow technical grounds having to do with California tax law that had nothing whatsoever to do with whether corporations were persons under the Fourteenth Amendment.

In fact, Harlan's decision begins by noting that since the Court could dispose of the case on other grounds, "it is not necessary to consider" whether the Fourteenth Amendment applies to corporations.[8]

It doesn't get more explicit: "it is not necessary to consider."

The Supreme Court explicitly refused to rule on corporate constitutional rights.

So where did the idea that *Santa Clara* established corporate constitutional rights come from?

The Headnote

J.C. Bancroft Davis was the Supreme Court's Reporter of Decisions, what we today call the court reporter. His job was to take notes and then publish the Court's written opinions in officially sanctioned volumes, adding brief headnotes to summarize each case.

For *Santa Clara*, Davis wrote: "The defendant Corporations are persons within the intent of the clause in section 1 of the Fourteenth Amendment to the Constitution of the United States, which forbids a state to deny to any person within its jurisdiction the equal protection of the laws."[9]

That sentence appears *before* the decision itself. It looks official. It's printed in the *United States Reports*, the official record of Supreme Court decisions.

But it's not part of the decision. It's not law; it's just Davis's statement. And Davis's statement directly contradicts what the decision actually says.

The decision itself said the Court was definitely not deciding the corporate constitutional rights question: it was "not necessary to consider" because they were only going to rule on whether the county illegally counted the value of fenceposts when calculating the value of the land for property taxes.

The headnote, on the other hand, explicitly says the Court decided that corporations are persons.

One of them was clearly and blatantly lying. And since the decision was the official ruling of the Supreme Court, written by Justice Harlan and agreed to by the other justices, the liar had to be Davis.

Davis, we now can see, put words in the Court's mouth—words the Court never said, using language that would alter the course of American history for more than a century.

The question is *why*?

The Cover-Up Begins

Within months of the publication of the *Santa Clara* decision, lawyers for corporations began citing it as precedent for corporate constitutional rights, pointing to the headnote instead of the decision.

Judges, seeing that citation in the official *United States Reports*, assumed it was accurate and, within a decade, began to rely on it. Soon, other cases were citing *Santa Clara* as having finally and firmly established that corporations are persons under the Fourteenth Amendment and entitled to the rights previously enjoyed only by humans.

Nobody, it appears, bothered to check the actual decision. Why would they? After all, it was right there in the official record, summarized by the Supreme Court's own official reporter, a wealthy and powerful man with a well-known reputation who was the son of the Massachusetts governor.

In 1889, just three years after *Santa Clara*, corporate lawyers first successfully established that damnable headnote as precedent. In *Minneapolis & St. Louis Railway Co. v. Beckwith*, the Supreme Court cited *Santa Clara*, claiming in an actual decision that corporations are persons under the Fourteenth Amendment.

With that case, now in an actual decision by the Court itself and not just a statement by the Court's reporter, the lie became the law.

And today, much to the detriment of both democracy and America's working class, 137 years later, it still is.

What Was Lost

The fraud of 1886 didn't just corrupt constitutional law. It altered the entire course of American history.

The Progressive Era still happened, and the labor movement still won important victories. The income tax was established. Antitrust laws were passed. Women won the right to vote. The First Progressive Era, from the 1890s through 1920, identified crucial reforms, most of which just made America's oligarchs even more determined to fight back.

And when the Republican Great Depression showed what unrestrained corporate power really meant—banks failing, families starving, millions homeless—Franklin Roosevelt reinvented American politics and economics to create the Second Progressive Era, what he called the New Deal. It included Social Security, the right to organize unions, regulations that prevented banks from gambling with depositors' money, and a tax system that required the wealthy to pay their fair share.

By 1981 when Reagan was sworn into office, the American Dream was real for fully two-thirds of Americans. A single income could support a family. You could buy a house for three times your annual salary. College was affordable or, in some states, even free. Healthcare didn't bankrupt families. Retirement was secure. Children had better opportunities than their parents.[10]

But throughout that entire period, Field's and Davis's doctrine of corporate constitutional rights remained embedded in constitutional law like a dormant virus or an unexploded landmine. The oligarchs had lost battle after battle during the Progressive Eras, but they succeeded in hanging onto their ultimate weapon: the fraudulent claim that corporations had constitutional rights.

When Ronald Reagan's "conservative (neoliberal oligarchic) revolution" began in 1981, that weapon was activated. Corporate constitutional rights became the battering ram that destroyed the American Dream, piece by piece, decade by decade, until we arrived at today, when Millennials own just 4.6 percent of the nation's wealth compared to the 21.3 percent Boomers owned at the same age, and our president is openly dancing to the tunes of major polluters and fossil fuel corporations in exchange for campaign contributions and gifts.[11]

The railroad oligarchs and their shills of 1886, J.C. Bancroft Davis and Stephen J. Field, planted a bomb in the Constitution. It took five generations to fully detonate it, but when the oligarchs of the 1970s and 1980s finally did, it laid waste to almost everything the Progressive Eras had built.[12]

Understanding how that bomb was planted—and who planted it—is critical to knowing how to defuse it.

That's what brings us to the triggerman: J.C. Bancroft Davis.

The Crime Scene

How Corporations Stole Human Rights in 1886

THE CASE

Santa Clara County v. Southern Pacific Railroad Company,
US Supreme Court, 1886

Actual issue: A county sued a railroad over $30,000 in unpaid property taxes.

THE CONSPIRATORS

THE TRIGGERMAN: **J.C. Bancroft Davis**, Supreme Court Reporter
Former railroad president • Railroad stock owner

His crime: Wrote a fraudulent summary claiming the Court ruled corporations are "persons"

THE MASTERMIND: **Justice Stephen J. Field**, Supreme Court Justice
Railroad stock owner • Friend of railroad oligarchs

His goal: Corporate constitutional rights through decades of failed court cases

THE FRAUD

WHAT DAVIS WROTE
(The Headnote)

"The defendant Corporations are persons within the intent of the Fourteenth Amendment…"

THIS IS NOT LAW
Headnotes are summaries with no legal standing.

WHAT THE COURT ACTUALLY RULED
"It is not necessary to consider" *whether the Fourteenth Amendment applies to corporations.*

THE COURT REFUSED TO DECIDE
They ruled only on a technicality about fence taxes.

THE RESULT

For 140 years, courts cited Davis's fraudulent headnote as if it were law.

One lie became the foundation for

- † *Citizens United*: corporate "free speech" to buy elections
- † *Hobby Lobby*: corporate "religious freedom"
- † Corporate "privacy" to hide pollution and crimes
- † Corporate "due process" to block regulations

**The Supreme Court never ruled that corporations are people.
A court reporter made it up.**

Source: Santa Clara County v. Southern Pacific Railroad Company, 118 US 394 (1886)

2

The Courtroom Showdown

THE OLD SENATE CHAMBER IN WASHINGTON WAS WARM FOR JANUARY, the heavy air thick with coal smoke and anticipation. On January 26, 1886, two men prepared to argue before the most powerful court in America. One represented the largest corporation on the continent. The other represented a small California county fighting to collect its taxes.

The outcome would shape American democracy for the next century and a half.

The Railroad's Champion

S.W. Sanderson entered the chamber like a man who owned it. And in a sense, he did. The chief legal counsel for the Southern Pacific Railroad stood more than six feet tall, an aristocratic bear of a man with neatly combed gray hair and an elegantly trimmed white goatee. For more than two decades, Sanderson had made himself rich litigating for the nation's largest railroads, defending the interests of oligarchs like Leland Stanford, Charles Crocker, Collis Huntington, and Mark Hopkins.

Sanderson was famous enough that artist Thomas Hill had included him in his painting *The Last Spike*, commemorating the 1869 transcontinental meeting of the Union Pacific and Central Pacific Railroads at Promontory Summit, Utah. In that painting, Sanderson appears portentous and dignified, standing among the railroad barons who had conquered a continent. He saw himself as their equal.

That day he would ask the Supreme Court to grant his corporate clients something they had been seeking for decades: the constitutional rights of human beings.

Sanderson had argued versions of this claim before. The railroads had lost every time. In 1873, the Court had declared that the Fourteenth Amendment's "one pervading purpose" was "the freedom of the slave race." In 1877, the railroads brought four different cases to the Supreme Court, arguing that they deserved constitutional protection as "persons" under that same amendment. They lost all four.

But Sanderson kept coming back. The oligarchs he served had unlimited resources, unlimited patience, and unlimited ambition. They would keep filing cases until they found a way to win.

The People's Advocate

Santa Clara County's lawyer Delphin M. Delmas was everything Sanderson was not. Where Sanderson was large and imposing, Delmas was small and unimposing, a fastidious man known to wear a frock coat, gray-striped trousers, a wing collar, and an ascot tie. He had a substantial nose and a broad forehead only slightly covered with a wispy bit of thinning hair. He looked like a clerk, not a gladiator.

But in the courtroom, Delmas transformed. His voice thrummed with emotion. He was nationally known as the "master dramatist of America's courtrooms," and by 1904 would be called "the Silver-Tongued Orator of the West" when elected a delegate to the Democratic National Convention.

His courtroom performances were legendary. The nation would later learn just how brilliant he was in 1908, when he successfully defended Harry K. Thaw for murder in the most sensational case of the first half of the century, later made into the 1955 movie *The Girl in the Red Velvet Swing*, starring Ray Milland and Joan Collins. Luther Adler played Delmas.

But on this January day in 1886, Delmas was not yet famous. He was simply the young lead attorney for Santa Clara County, California, a small government entity suing the massive Southern Pacific Railroad for six years of unpaid property taxes.

While Sanderson had spent his career serving the richest men in America, Delmas had always worked on behalf of local governments and ordinary citizens. He had passionately argued, *pro bono*, before the California legislature for a law to protect the nation's last remaining redwood forests. He was fiercely defensive about the rights of natural persons, of actual human beings, against the artificial creatures of law that sought to usurp their place.

For Delmas, this case was about something far larger than taxes. It was about whether corporations created by state law could claim the constitutional rights won by flesh-and-blood human beings who had fought and died for independence and then triumphed over the South's brutal oligarchs in the Civil War.

The Stakes

The case itself was almost comically trivial. The Southern Pacific Railroad owed Santa Clara County approximately $30,000 in back taxes on property with a $30 million mortgage. That's like having a $10,000 car and refusing to pay a $10 tax on it, then taking the case all the way to the Supreme Court.

One of the railroad's defenses was even more absurd: when the state assessed the value of the railroad's property, it had accidentally included the value of fences built by private landowners along the right-of-way. The county, not the state, should have separately assessed those fences. Therefore, the railroad argued, the tax was "unequal" compared to what they paid in other counties.

But the railroad's lawyers had slipped something else into their arguments, something that had nothing to do with fences or tax assessments. They claimed that the railroad corporation was a "person" under the Fourteenth Amendment, entitled to the same constitutional protections as the freed slaves that amendment was written to protect.

If the Court agreed, it would transform American law. Corporations would gain the power to challenge any regulation, any tax, any democratic decision that treated them differently from human citizens. They would gain access to the Bill of Rights, to due process, to equal protection.

They would become, in the eyes of the Constitution, the equals of the human beings who'd created them.

Sanderson's Argument

Sanderson rose to address the Court. Chief Justice Morrison Waite looked down from the bench, a square-headed man with a bristly graying beard that shot out in every direction. Waite himself was a former railroad attorney who had never served as a judge before being appointed Chief Justice. He owed his position to President Grant, whose administration was so wracked with railroad bribery scandals that his own Republican Party refused to renominate him for the presidency.

"I believe," Sanderson declared, "that the clause of the Fourteenth Amendment in relation to equal protection means the same thing as the plain and simple yet sublime words found in our Declaration of Independence: 'all men are created equal.' Not equal in physical or mental power, not equal in fortune or social position, but equal before the law."[13]

It was audacious. Sanderson was claiming that a railroad corporation, an artificial entity created by state law and owned by some of the richest oligarchs in America, deserved the same constitutional protections as freed slaves emerging from centuries of bondage. He was hijacking the language of liberation to serve the interests of concentrated wealth.

Sanderson's fellow lawyer for the railroads, George F. Edmunds, added that the Fourteenth Amendment created a "broad and catholic provision for universal security, resting upon citizenship as it regarded political rights, and resting upon humanity as it regarded private rights."[14]

Humanity. The railroad lawyers were claiming their corporate clients were human.

Delmas Responds

When Delmas rose to speak, his transformation began. The small, fastidious man became something else entirely—a prophet of democratic rage: "The defendant claims that California's taxation policy violates that portion of the Fourteenth Amendment which provides that no state shall deny to any person within its jurisdiction the equal protection of the laws," Delmas began, his voice thrumming with barely controlled fury. Such an argument, he said, "if tenable, would place the organic law of California in a position ridiculous to the extreme."[15]

Then Delmas went on the attack:

> The shield behind which the Southern Pacific Railroad attacks the Constitution and laws of California is the Fourteenth Amendment. It argues that the amendment guarantees to every person within the jurisdiction of the State the equal protection of the laws; that a corporation is a person; that, therefore, it must receive the same protection as that accorded to all other persons in like circumstances.... To my mind, the fallacy of the argument lies in the assumption that corporations are entitled to be governed by the laws that are applicable to natural persons.

Delmas reached for the ultimate authority, the book that the Founders themselves had consulted when writing the Constitution: Sir William Blackstone's 1765 *Commentaries on the Laws of England*. He quoted Blackstone: "Persons are divided by the law into either natural persons or artificial. Natural persons are such as the God of nature formed us; artificial are such as are created and devised by human laws for the purposes of society and government, which are called corporations or bodies politic."

Delmas moved from legal authority to common sense. If a corporation was truly a "person," why could it not make out a will or get married?

"This definition suggests at once that though a corporation is a person, it is not the same kind of person as a human being, and need not, nay, in the very nature of things, cannot enjoy all the rights of such or be governed by the same laws. When the law says, 'Any person being of sound mind and of the age of discretion may make a will,' or 'any person having arrived at the age of majority may marry,' I presume the most ardent advocate of equality of protection would hardly contend that corporations must enjoy the right of testamentary disposition or of contracting matrimony."[16]

The Heart of the Matter

Now Delmas reached the heart of his argument. Everyone in that chamber knew the history of the Fourteenth Amendment. It had been written to protect freed slaves, to ensure that the men and women who had been held in bondage would have the same rights as their former masters. The blood of a civil war was still fresh on the ground. The memory of slavery was still alive.

He continued: "The whole history of the Fourteenth Amendment demonstrates beyond dispute that its whole scope and object was to establish equality between men, an attainable result, and not to establish equality between natural and artificial beings, an impossible result."

Delmas was trembling now, his small frame vibrating with righteous indignation. He was a California Democrat who had spent his life fighting for the little guy, and he knew, as did anyone who read the newspapers of that era, exactly what the Fourteenth Amendment meant and why it had been written.

The Fourteenth Amendment, he declared, "is as broad as humanity itself":

> Wherever man is found within the confines of this Union, whatever his race, religion, or color, be he Caucasian, African, or Mongolian, be he Christian, infidel, or idolater, be he white, black, or copper-colored, he may take shelter under this great law as under a shield against individual oppression in any form, individual injustice in any shape. It is a protection to all men because they are men, members of the same great family, children of the same omnipotent Creator.
>
> In its comprehensive words I find written by the hand of a nation of sixty millions in the firmament of imperishable law the sentiment uttered more than a hundred years ago by the philosopher of Geneva, and re-echoed in this country by the authors of the Declaration of the Thirteen Colonies: Proclaim to the world the equality of man.

The Mission of the Amendment

Speaking of the object of the Fourteenth Amendment, Delmas laid it out plain:

> Its mission was to raise the humble, the down-trodden, and the oppressed to the level of the most exalted upon the broad plain of humanity, to make man the equal of man; but not to make the creature of the State, the bodiless,

soulless, and mystic creature called a corporation, the equal of the creature of God....

Therefore, I venture to repeat that the Fourteenth Amendment does not command equality between human beings and corporations.

The bodiless, soulless, and mystic creature called a corporation. Delmas had found the phrase that captured exactly what the railroads were asking for: to make an artificial creation of law the constitutional equal of a child of God.

The Warning

In closing, Delmas issued a warning. This case, he suggested, could be one of the most important in the history of the United States. If corporations were given the powerful cudgel of human rights secured by the Bill of Rights, their ability to amass wealth and power could lead to death, war, and the impoverishment of actual human beings on a massive scale.

"I have now done," he said. "Yet I cannot but think that the controversy now debated before your Honors is one of no ordinary importance."

The chamber fell silent. Delmas had laid before the Court the full stakes of what the railroad was asking. He had traced the history of the Fourteenth Amendment from the American Revolution to the blood of the Civil War to this moment, from Declaration of Independence to the liberation of enslaved human beings to the attempted liberation of soulless corporations.

The question was whether the Court would listen.

The Long Wait

A year and five months passed while the Supreme Court debated the issues in private.

In that time, the railroad oligarchs waited. Leland Stanford continued expanding his empire. Collis Huntington continued buying politicians. The Southern Pacific Railroad continued to refuse to pay its taxes, its lawyers confident that their strategy would eventually succeed.

And then came May 10, 1886.

That afternoon, in the same Old Senate Chamber where Delmas had delivered his passionate defense of human rights, Chief Justice Waite prepared to announce the Court's decision. Delmas was there. Sanderson was there. The fate of American democracy hung in the balance.

What happened next would not become clear for another eighty years. The crime was about to be committed, and it would be hidden in plain sight for generations.

Delmas had won the argument. He would lose the war.

A Discovery Across Time

I searched for the better part of a year for copies of the arguments made in the *Santa Clara* case. The Supreme Court kept no detailed notes of oral arguments in those days. Most of what was said in that chamber was lost to history.

Then, in an antiquarian bookstore in San Francisco, I found a treasure: *Speeches and Addresses by D.M. Delmas*. It was a hardbound collection that Delmas had personally paid to self-publish in 1901, containing his most important courtroom arguments, including his full presentation before the Supreme Court in the *Santa Clara* case.

Holding that book was like holding a time machine. Delmas's arguments were as brilliant and persuasive as any words that Erle Stanley Gardner ever put into the mouth of Perry Mason. Here was the voice of a man fighting for the soul of American democracy, preserved across more than a century.

He was right about everything. Corporations were artificial creations of law, not natural persons. The Fourteenth Amendment was written to protect freed slaves, not railroad barons. Granting corporations constitutional rights would distort American democracy for generations to come. It could even empower a would-be dictator to take over America with the help of corporate money.

Delmas saw it all, warned of it all, fought against it with every tool at his disposal.

And he lost anyway. Not because his arguments were wrong, but because the fix was already in. The conspiracy was already underway.

What Delmas could not know, standing in that courtroom, was that Justice Stephen J. Field was sitting on the bench with a plan. Field had already ruled repeatedly (including in the *Santa Clara* case) as a circuit court judge in California that corporations were persons under the Fourteenth Amendment. He owned railroad stock. He socialized with railroad executives. He harbored presidential ambitions that he hoped the oligarchs would finance.

And he had a friend in the court reporter's office.

3

The Triggerman

J.C. Bancroft Davis

Who was J.C. Bancroft Davis? And why would he commit such an audacious fraud?

The answer lies in his connections to the railroad oligarchs, his own ambitions within America's elite power structure, and—most importantly—whose interests he was really serving when he wrote that fraudulent headnote.

Davis wasn't just helping the Southern Pacific Railroad win a tax case. He was helping an entire class of oligarchs acquire a constitutional weapon they could use against democracy itself, against the Progressive Era reforms that threatened their power, against the labor movement that demanded dignity for workers, and ultimately against every democratic effort to build what would later be called the American Dream.

The Court Reporter

John Chandler Bancroft Davis was born into privilege in 1822. His father was a prominent Massachusetts politician. Young Bancroft—he went by his middle name—attended Harvard, studied law, and entered a career that would take him through journalism, diplomacy, and ultimately to the Supreme Court.

By 1883, when he became the Supreme Court's Reporter of Decisions, Davis was sixty-one years old. He'd served as Assistant Secretary of State, negotiated treaties, argued cases before the Supreme Court, and moved comfortably in the highest circles of American power.

He was also heavily invested in railroads, and had briefly been the president of a small railroad on the east coast.

Davis owned railroad stock, had financial relationships with railroad companies, and his social circle included railroad executives and oligarchs. When he took the job as Supreme Court Reporter, he brought those connections with him.[17]

The Reporter's job was supposed to be purely administrative: record the decisions, write brief summaries, publish the volumes. It wasn't supposed to involve making law.

But Davis saw an opportunity.

A Man of His Class

To understand Davis, you have to understand the world he inhabited. The 1880s were the Gilded Age, a time when a small number of oligarchs controlled vast portions of America's wealth while most workers lived in poverty, children labored in factories, women had no rights or political power, and democratic governance was routinely corrupted by corporate money.

Davis moved in the circles of those oligarchs. He dined with them. He invested with them. He shared their worldview: that property rights were sacred, that democratic regulation was tyranny, that the wealthy deserved protection from the masses.

This wasn't unusual for men of his class. What was unusual, though, was his position. As the Supreme Court's official reporter, Davis had access to the official record of constitutional law. He could shape how decisions were understood, cited, and applied.

And the railroad oligarchs and their man on the Court, Stephen J. Field, needed someone in exactly that position. Whether they recruited him explicitly or whether he simply understood what was expected of a man in his station, Davis delivered.

The Mysterious Letter

In 1886, after writing his fraudulent headnote but before publication, Davis wrote to Chief Justice Morrison Waite. The letter has been preserved in Waite's papers at the Library of Congress, and I don't think anybody had seen it in a century before I initiated an investigation and discovered it in a dust-covered file.

Davis wrote: "I have a memorandum in the California Cases *Santa Clara County v. Southern Pacific R.R. Co.* as follows. In opening, the Court stated that it did not wish to hear argument on the question whether the Fourteenth Amendment applies to such corporations as are parties in these suits. All the Judges were of the opinion that it does."[18]

Davis was asking Waite to confirm that his summary was accurate, that Waite had indeed announced from the bench that corporations were persons under the Fourteenth Amendment, and that all the justices agreed.

Waite's response, also preserved in his papers, is remarkable.

Waite wrote back: "I think your mem. in the California Railroad Tax cases expresses with sufficient accuracy what was said before the argument began. I leave it with you to determine whether anything need be said about it in the report inasmuch as we avoided meeting the constitutional question in the decision."

And there it is. Waite confirmed that something was said before argument began, but he also noted that the Court "avoided meeting the constitutional question in the decision."

In other words, even if Waite made some random comment before oral arguments began (and we'll examine whether he really did in a moment), the Court's actual decision explicitly did not rule on corporate constitutional rights other than to reject them as the basis for a decision.

Waite wrote that he left it to Davis "to determine whether anything need be said about it [the corporate constitutional rights argument] in the report." That's a remarkable delegation of authority. The Chief Justice was letting the court reporter decide what to include in the official record.

And Davis took that opportunity to include in his headnote the bizarre claim that the Court had ruled on corporate constitutional rights, even though the decision itself said no such thing.

What Actually Happened?

Did Waite really make that announcement before oral arguments? Did all the justices really agree that corporations were persons?

The historical evidence suggests neither occurred.

First, there's no record of such an announcement in the official transcript of oral arguments.

Second, the decision itself contradicts it. If all the justices agreed that corporations were persons and thus entitled to the protections of the Fourteenth Amendment, why would Justice Harlan write that "it is not necessary to consider" that question? Why would the Court avoid the issue entirely?

Third, no other justices left any record whatsoever of agreeing to such a radical position. We have their papers, their letters, their other opinions, and none of them suggest they believed at that time that corporations were constitutional persons for purposes of Fourteenth Amendment protections.

And fourth, the timing is suspicious. If Waite had actually made this announcement in the context Davis was suggesting, it would have been big news. Contemporary newspaper accounts of the case don't mention it, and legal commentators at the time didn't note it. It only appears in Davis's headnote, which was written months after the decision as Waite lay sick and dying from heart failure.

The most likely explanation is that Waite had said something to that effect about corporations being a kind of *artificial person*. As Blackstone noted a century earlier and Delmas quoted, it's true that corporations have some constitutional rights: they need legal standing to own property, pay taxes, open bank accounts, be held responsible under the law, and so on, and that's been recognized by the Supreme Court going all the way back to the *Dartmouth v. Woodward* decision in 1819.

But the artificial person that's a corporation is an entirely different thing from the "natural persons" the Fourteenth Amendment was written to protect. So, it's possible that Waite was simply acknowledging *Dartmouth*, if he did make that comment or something close to it.

Thus, either Davis manufactured the claim or he mischaracterized something Waite said. Either way, Davis put it in the official record as if corporations having rights similar to humans was now established law.

And because Davis was the official reporter, because his headnote appeared in *United States Reports*, because nobody had reason to doubt it, the fraud succeeded.

The Motive

This raises the inevitable questions: Why would Davis do this? What did he gain?

The answer is most likely found in the gilded world of 1880s America, where oligarchs lavishly rewarded those who best served their interests, much as Trump does today with his corporate donors when they bring him gifts and donations.

Railroad stock holdings would increase in value if railroads gained constitutional protections from taxation and regulation, and Davis owned railroad stock (he'd even briefly been president of a regional railroad). He had friends who owned railroad stock, and the headnote served their interests directly.

But there was likely more to it than just money. Men like Davis operated in what were then referred to by social scientists as "networks of mutual benefit." Today we call it naked corruption. Back in those days, they simply called it "the way business gets done." You helped the railroad oligarchs, they helped you—financially, politically, and even socially.

Thus, Davis didn't need to be offered a direct bribe. He knew which side his bread was buttered on. Writing a headnote that served railroad interests cost him nothing and potentially gained him much.

It was the perfect crime: invisible, deniable, and enormously profitable for everyone except the American working class and the future generations that Reagan and the GOP would crush using Davis's headnote.

Serving the Oligarch Class

It also turns out that Davis's fraud served interests far beyond the Southern Pacific Railroad's tax case. He wasn't just helping one corporation avoid property taxes; he helped an entire oligarchic class acquire a weapon they could use against democracy for generations to come.

Consider what the oligarchs faced in 1886. The labor movement was growing. The Knights of Labor had just reached peak membership and became the largest union in world history. Strikes were spreading across industries. Workers were demanding the eight-hour day, a living wage, and safer working conditions.

States were beginning to seriously regulate corporations by setting safety standards, limiting working hours, and requiring fair treatment of workers. Farmers were organizing against railroad and processor monopolies. Reformers were demanding antitrust laws to break up corporate consolidation, and the newspapers were all over it.

The First Progressive Era was dawning, and everything the oligarchs had built through corruption, exploitation, and ruthless business practices was, in their minds, under threat.

What they needed was more than a simple court victory in one tax case: they needed a constitutional principle they could use to fight back against democratic governance itself. They wanted to be able to claim that common-sense regulations violated their constitutional rights, that taxes were unconstitutional "takings" as defined by the Fifth Amendment, and that the labor protections FDR would later codify into law infringed on their constitutional rights.

Corporate constitutional rights gave them exactly that and more.

With Davis's fraudulent headnote established as precedent, corporations could claim Fourteenth Amendment protections, such as "due process" rights. They could claim to be the victims of "unequal protection" prohibited by that Amendment when states tried to treat them differently from human beings.

Davis handed the oligarchs a constitutional weapon that they'd use for the next 140 years to fight against every democratic effort to build and protect the American Dream.

The Accomplice

But John Chandler Bancroft Davis didn't act alone. He had an accomplice on the Supreme Court itself: Justice Stephen J. Field.

Field was more than just sympathetic to corporate interests; he was a true believer in corporate constitutional rights. He'd been advocating for them in dissents and concurrences on behalf of the railroad oligarchs in California for years.

Justice Field and Court Reporter Davis knew each other well. They moved in the same elite social and political circles. They shared the same ideology: that property rights were sacred and democratic attempts to regulate corporations were tyrannical.

Justice Field had been waiting for the right case to establish corporate constitutional rights, and *Santa Clara* looked promising. But when the majority decided to rule on narrow technical grounds instead of reaching the constitutional question, Field's opportunity slipped away.

Or did it?

Reporter Davis's headnote accomplished what Justice Field couldn't achieve through the Court's decision. It established corporate constitutional rights in the official record, where future courts would cite it as precedent.

Did Justice Field encourage Davis to write the fraudulent headnote? Did they coordinate? The historical record doesn't prove conspiracy, but it shows opportunity, motive, and benefit.

What we know for certain is that Justice Field welcomed the headnote's impact. In later cases, he cited gleefully *Santa Clara* as establishing corporate constitutional rights, and he never corrected the record. He never bothered to say, "Wait, that's not what we decided."

The silence of accomplices often speaks loudly.

The Perfect Crime

By the time anyone might have noticed the fraud, it was too late. Less than four months after joining the Court in 1937, Justice Hugo Black issued a dissenting opinion in *Connecticut General Life Insurance Company v. Johnson*, writing:

> I do not believe the word "person" in the Fourteenth Amendment includes corporations.... Certainly, when the Fourteenth Amendment was submitted for approval, the people were not told that the states... ratified an amendment granting new and revolutionary rights to corporations.

> This amendment sought to prevent discrimination by the states against classes or races.... Yet, of the cases in this Court in which the Fourteenth Amendment was applied during the first fifty years after its adoption, less than one-half of 1 percent invoked it in protection of the Negro race, and more than 50 percent asked that its benefits be extended to corporations.

Courts subsequent to the publication of Davis's case summary had already relied on the headnote, so the precedent was established. Unwinding it would require admitting that the Supreme Court's official reporter had committed fraud and that generations of lawyers and judges had been fooled.

Nobody associated with the Supreme Court, and certainly nobody in corporate America, wanted to admit that.

So, the fraud has stood for a century and a half. It became law through repetition. By 1890, just four years after *Santa Clara*, even the Supreme Court itself was citing the headnote as if it were the decision.

The perfect crime isn't one that's never discovered: it's the one where discovery of it changes nothing, where the damage is already done, and where correcting the fraud would be more embarrassing or difficult than living with it.

Davis committed the perfect crime. The railroad oligarchs benefited tremendously, as do massive corporations and their billionaire owners today, but American democracy and the working class paid the price.

The Long Shadow of the Triggerman

Court Reporter J.C. Bancroft Davis died in 1907, twenty-one years after writing the fraudulent headnote that reshaped American democracy. He never faced consequences for what he did, was never investigated, prosecuted, or even publicly questioned about it.

He probably died believing he'd done nothing wrong, or at least nothing that men of his class and position didn't routinely do. Helping the oligarchs was simply what one did back then; it was how the system worked.

But the shadow of his fraud now stretches across more than a century:

> † Every time a corporation claims First Amendment rights to spend unlimited money on elections, it's Davis's fraud.
>
> † Every time a corporation claims due process rights to block environmental regulations, it's Davis's fraud.
>
> † Every time a corporation claims equal protection to avoid taxes that fund schools, roads, and public services, it's Davis's fraud.
>
> † Every time a corporation claims religious freedom to deny employees healthcare coverage, it's Davis's fraud.
>
> † Every time a corporation prevents the EPA from investigating their pollution by citing the Fourth Amendment right to privacy, it's Davis's fraud.

The American middle class that Reaganomics shrank from 66 percent in 1981 to 43 percent today was crushed under Davis's fraud.[19]

The fifty-plus trillion dollars transferred from working Americans into billionaires' money bins since the Reagan Revolution was enabled by Davis's fraud.

The student debt, the healthcare bankruptcies, the housing crisis, the stagnant wages, the dying American Dream: all were made possible by that single fraudulent sentence written by a court reporter serving the railroad oligarchs' interests in 1886.

Digging one level deeper, however, we find that while Davis was the triggerman, he was also apparently working for someone else. To understand the full scope of the conspiracy, we must understand its mastermind: Justice Stephen J. Field.

4

The Mastermind

Supreme Court Justice Stephen J. Field

IF J.C. BANCROFT DAVIS WAS THE TRIGGERMAN, THEN JUSTICE STEPHEN Johnson Field was the mastermind behind the corporate theft of constitutional rights. He'd spent three decades on the Supreme Court, building the intellectual infrastructure that would transform corporations into constitutional persons.

We must understand Justice Field to clearly see how democracy was hijacked by the oligarchs of that era. But more than just that, understanding Field also reveals the ideology behind the hijacking. This wasn't just a case of corruption or greed, although there was plenty of both. This was, instead, a vision of America fundamentally opposed to the Founders' and Framers' vision of America and explicitly at odds with the possibility of creating a thriving middle class.

Field, like the railroad oligarchs to whom he was beholden, believed that property rights always trumped human rights. He believed the wealthy deserved constitutional protection from what John Adams called "the rabble": the democratic majorities, the "common people." He believed that workers organizing for better wages, farmers demanding fair treatment from the railroads they needed for their survival, and states regulating corporate behavior were all forms of tyranny against the morbidly rich of his day.

His vision was thus essentially feudal: a small class of white male property owners should rule over everyone else, protected by constitutional rights that the democratic majority could never touch.

Corporate constitutional rights were the weapon he—and the oligarchs close to him—chose to make that vision real.

The Gold Rush Justice

Stephen Field arrived in California in 1849, just as gold fever swept the territory. He wasn't, however, looking for gold in the ground. He made his considerable fortune in lawyers' fees, land speculation, and by exploiting and supporting raw political power.

Field established himself as a lawyer in Marysville, then became the *alcalde* for the town, a title encompassing the combination of mayor, judge, and local potentate inherited from California's Mexican period. He wielded power arbitrarily, frequently jailed his more outspoken critics, and almost always ruled in favor of those clients who paid him well.

When California became a state, Field joined the state legislature, then became a justice on the California Supreme Court. He was ruthless, ambitious, and utterly convinced that rich people and their corporations were the only ones that really mattered.

In 1863, President Lincoln appointed Field to the US Supreme Court. It was a political appointment, as Lincoln needed California's support and Field's Democratic credentials to help balance the Court (with the bonus that he wasn't, like the Southern Democrats, a slaveholder).

Lincoln would later regret his appointment, as Field quickly became one of the most consequential justices in American history, and not in a good way.

The Ideology of Oligarchy

Field brought to the Supreme Court a fully formed ideology that would reshape American law: corporations were property, property was sacred under the Constitution, and any democratic attempts to regulate or even "excessively" tax property were simple tyranny.

This wasn't capitalism in any way Adam Smith would have recognized. Smith, in both *Theory of Moral Sentiments* and *Wealth of Nations,* advocated competitive markets and warned against monopolies that conspired against small competitors and the public. Field, on the other hand, pushed for corporate power and saw democratic regulation of business activity as the enemy.

Field's ideology came from his experience in California. He'd seen and admired vigilante justice, rough-and-tumble mining camps, and the rapid accumulation of massive fortunes. As an attorney, he'd watched the railroad oligarchs build an empire, and as a judge had become invested in their success.

Most importantly, he agreed with that era's oligarchs (who were often murdering labor leaders) that the wealthy deserved protection from the democratic majority. The "mob" couldn't be trusted with power, particularly the power to tax or regulate the railroads. Property owners, especially corporate property owners, needed constitutional shields against populist politicians.

The Fourteenth Amendment, he hoped, would finally give Field his opportunity to repay decades of largesse from the nation's richest men.

Field's War Against the Emerging Middle Class

Field wasn't just pushing corporate rights in the abstract. He was waging war against the emerging American Dream even before it could be named or fully take shape.

During Field's time on the Court, workers were organizing into unions, demanding living wages that would allow them to support families, buy homes, and give their children opportunities they never had. Farmers were forming cooperatives to escape the stranglehold of railroad monopolies. Small businesses were fighting against corporate consolidation that threatened to crush them.

States responded positively to these deeply popular movements by passing laws limiting working hours, requiring safe working conditions, preventing monopolistic practices, and taxing corporate wealth to fund public schools and infrastructure.

Every one of those laws threatened Field's oligarchic vision of America. Every one weakened the power of the oligarchs and gave it to democratic majorities. Every one moved America closer to what FDR would later call a nation where poor and working class "necessitous men" could become "free men."

Field saw all of this as a "dictatorship of the proletariat," a dangerous move toward the hot new idea of Marxism that was then sweeping the world's intelligentsia.[20] He believed that workers demanding fair wages was simple theft from property owners. He saw states regulating corporations as an unconstitutional interference with property rights and the democratic majority asserting control over economic life as mob rule.

Corporate constitutional rights were Field's legal weapon against the American Dream before it could fully emerge.

Rewriting Reconstruction

The Fourteenth Amendment was meant to protect freed slaves, but Field believed it could be used to a different purpose: protecting corporations from state regulation.

Starting in the 1870s, Justice Field began writing dissents in both the 9th Circuit and the Supreme Court arguing that corporations were persons under the Fourteenth Amendment. He lost those arguments repeatedly as the majority of the Court understood what the Fourteenth Amendment was actually for, and several—including Waite—even occasionally ridiculed Field as a "man obsessed."[21]

But Field was patient. He knew that the Supreme Court's composition would change with time. He knew that repeating an argument often enough can make it seem reasonable. And he knew that corporate money would fund challenges to every regulation, every tax, and every democratic attempt to constrain corporate power, and he wanted that money behind him and his presidential aspirations.

Field was playing the long game, building an intellectual framework that future courts could adopt.

The Slaughterhouse Dissent

In 1873, in the *Slaughterhouse Cases*, Field wrote one of the most important dissents in American legal history. It was important not because it was right, but because it laid the groundwork for what would later be called corporate constitutional rights.

The case involved the state of Louisiana granting a statewide monopoly to one single slaughterhouse in New Orleans owned by one of that state's wealthiest men. Small and independent butchers sued, claiming their Fourteenth Amendment "equal protection" rights were violated.

The majority on the Supreme Court ruled against the independent butchers by throwing out the Fourteenth Amendment argument. Justice Samuel Miller, writing for the Court, explained that the Fourteenth Amendment was "designed to assure to the colored race the enjoyment of all the civil rights that under the law are enjoyed by white persons." It wasn't, in other words, ever meant to revolutionize federal–state relations or create new property rights.

Field dissented furiously. He argued that the Fourteenth Amendment protected broad economic rights, including the right to pursue any lawful occupation without government interference.

This argument of Field's was eventually adopted by the Court and became known as "substantive due process," the idea that the Due Process Clause of the Fourteenth Amendment protects not just fair procedures, but also certain fundamental rights from government interference.

It was a radical reinterpretation of the Fourteenth Amendment. And it was exactly what corporations needed to argue for constitutional protection from regulation.

Building the Case

Through the 1870s and 1880s, Justice Field kept pushing. In dissent after dissent, opinion after opinion, he argued that corporate property rights deserved constitutional protection, that corporations were persons, and that democratic regulation was, to use his word, tyranny.

The railroad oligarchs noticed and jumped aboard, funding legal challenges designed to reach Field's Court with a fact pattern that would fit with his worldview. They hired the best lawyers money could buy and cultivated relationships with sympathetic judges.

Field was thus their champion on the Court. He socialized with railroad executives, owned railroad stock, and traveled on private railroad cars. The conflicts of interest were obvious and enormous, but in that era were frequently overlooked.

In a later time, Field would have been forced to recuse himself from cases involving the railroads. But in the 1880s, much like with today's Roberts Court, judicial ethics were whatever the Court's judges said they were. Field, therefore, had no intention of recusing himself from the cases that mattered most to his ideology, his future political ambitions, and his investment portfolio.

The *Santa Clara* Set-Up

When the *Santa Clara* case reached the Supreme Court in 1886, Field saw his moment.

The case wasn't perfect, by any means. The legal issues were technical and boring, involving fence valuations and tax procedures. But it involved the railroad, whose very well-paid lawyer Sanderson was willing to argue the Fourteenth Amendment, and it thus gave Justice Field an opportunity to finally, after all those years of effort, establish a legal basis for corporate constitutional rights that would endure for more than a century.

Field's biggest problem, however, was that the majority of the Court didn't agree with him. They were skeptical of his Fourteenth Amendment arguments and generally preferred to rule on narrow grounds and—unlike today's corrupt Republican-dominated Court—generally tried to avoid constitutional questions altogether.

Field, then, couldn't control the majority. But he *could* influence the Court's official reporter.

J.C. Bancroft Davis and Stephen Field shared more than ideology. They were friends who socialized in the same circles. They both had financial interests in railroad stock. And they both believed corporations and the oligarchs who owned railroads deserved constitutional protections that went far beyond those applied to average working people.

Did Field simply come out and tell Davis to write a fraudulent headnote? While possible, the historical record doesn't prove a direct conspiracy. But it does show how opportunity, alignment of interest, and mutual benefit all came together that day in 1886.

What we know for certain is that after Davis wrote the headnote, Field never objected. In subsequent cases, in fact, Field *cited* the *Santa Clara* headnote as proof positive his Court had established corporate constitutional rights. He'd gotten what he wanted, even if he couldn't pull it off through the Court's actual decision.

The Long Shadow

Field stayed on the Supreme Court until 1897, becoming the second-longest-serving justice in American history at that time. His final years on the Court were marked by senility and bitterness, but his ideology had won.

By the late 1890s, the Court was regularly citing *Santa Clara* as precedent for corporate constitutional rights. Field's dissents became majority opinions, and his radical reinterpretation of the Fourteenth Amendment became settled law.

And the freed slaves for whom the Fourteenth Amendment was written? By 1896, in *Plessy v. Ferguson*, the Supreme Court ruled that "separate but equal" was constitutional, setting up more than a half-century of legal discrimination and apartheid.

Justice Henry Billings Brown's opinion in that case acknowledged that the post–Civil War amendments made Black people citizens and forbade states from denying equal protection, but insisted the Fourteenth was meant to secure legal/political equality, not to abolish "distinctions based upon color" or to require "social equality."[22]

The Fourteenth Amendment—which was supposed to protect Black Americans from discrimination—was instead used to uphold segregation.

Meanwhile, corporations flourished under Fourteenth Amendment protection. By 1900, the Supreme Court had ruled in favor of corporations claiming Fourteenth Amendment rights in dozens of cases. The amendment meant to serve freed slaves now mainly served to free corporations from democratic control by local, state, or even agencies of the federal government.

Field's transformation of American law was complete. The oligarchs had won, and democracy and the emerging American middle class had lost.

And it all traced back to that one fraudulent headnote in that one infamous 1886 case.

Field's Feudal Vision Realized

Field died in 1899, two years after leaving the Court. He'd spent thirty-four years as a Supreme Court justice. He'd reshaped American constitutional law more profoundly than almost any other jurist in history.

And he'd done it in service of a feudal vision that most Americans would have rejected if they'd understood it clearly.

His vision was the opposite of the American Dream that promised that hard work would be rewarded, ordinary people could build secure lives, and children would have more opportunities than their parents. Field's vision, instead, promised that the wealthy would stay wealthy, the powerful would stay powerful, and democratic majorities would be powerless to change anything.

For fifty years after Field's death, his vision seemed to triumph. The Gilded Age gave way to the Roaring Twenties, another era of oligarchic excess. Corporate power again grew unchecked, and wealth again concentrated at the top. Workers were again crushed when they tried to organize, and the American Dream began to seem like a cruel joke.

Then came the Great Crash of October 1929 and the Republican Great Depression. Field's America, the oligarchs' America, had collapsed under the weight of its own contradictions, excesses, and naked thefts.

President Franklin D. Roosevelt built a new and different America on the wreckage, where workers could organize, corporations were regulated for the public good, and the morbidly rich paid their fair share. We became, for the first time in the history of the world, a country where two-thirds of families could achieve the middle class by 1980.

But Roosevelt couldn't undo Justice Field's constitutional legacy empowered by court reporter Davis's headnote. Corporate constitutional rights remained embedded in the law, a then largely dormant weapon waiting to be activated. Thus, when Ronald Reagan's "Revolution" began in 1981, that weapon was turned against everything Roosevelt had built, and Donald Trump and the GOP are doubling down on it today.

After forty-plus years of Republican and neoliberal Democratic rule, Field's feudal vision is ascendant again today. Three men own more wealth than the bottom half of America combined. Corporations claim constitutional rights to buy elections, block regulations, and crush workers. And the American Dream is dying.

Stephen Field would be pleased, if not giddy: this is exactly what he wanted.

But Field and Davis didn't invent the idea of corporate constitutional rights out of nothing. Instead, they built on decades of corporate legal strategy. To understand how deeply rooted this fraud really is, we need to take a quick look at the seventy-year legal war that preceded *Santa Clara*.

5

The Seventy-Year Legal War

THE STORY OF THE BATTLES BOTH FOR AND AGAINST CORPORATE constitutional rights didn't begin in 1886. For seventy years before the *Santa Clara* non-decision, corporations fought a relentless legal war to gain access to the same constitutional rights the Founders and Framers intended exclusively for humans. They lost battle after battle until, with Davis and Field, the railroad oligarchs finally found a way to win by fraud.

Once we understand this, it's easy to see that corporate constitutional rights were never an accident or a misunderstanding: the doctrine was, instead, the result of a sustained, deliberate campaign by morbidly rich interests to acquire constitutional weapons they could use against the "mob rule" of democratic governance. The railroad and other American oligarchs tried honest arguments for seven decades, but, when that failed, they turned to fraud.

This history also shows exactly what the oligarchs were fighting against: virtually every reform that would later build—and today sustains—the American Dream and the social democracy that made it possible.

The Early Republic and Corporate Charters

Queen Elizabeth I created the first modern limited liability corporation— the British East India Company—in 1601, but by the time America was founded, corporations were still rare and tightly controlled. The Founders had fought a revolution against the British East India Company's economic and legal tyranny, and they weren't about to allow that kind of corporate power in their new republic.

In the early 1800s, corporations were only created by special acts of state legislatures. Each charter was a custom document specifying exactly what the corporation could do, how long it could exist, and what restrictions on its behavior applied.

A corporation chartered to build a toll bridge, for example, couldn't just suddenly decide to buy or open a bank. A textile mill corporation couldn't invest in railroads. Charters specified purpose, duration, capitalization, and governance. They could be revoked if the corporation "violated the public interest," an event called "the corporate death penalty," and frequently were dissolved this way.

That wasn't capitalism being stifled: it was democracy controlling its own creations for the benefit of the nation and its citizens.

As Thomas Jefferson warned in 1816: "I hope we shall crush in its birth the aristocracy of our moneyed corporations, which dare already to challenge our government to a trial of strength and bid defiance to the laws of our country."

The Founders understood what we seem to have forgotten: corporations are not natural beings like you and me. Instead, they're legal fictions created by government to serve public purposes. By the standards of the Declaration of Independence ("Life, liberty, and the pursuit of happiness") and the Constitution, they have no inherent rights, only privileges granted them by We the People via the state governments that chartered them.

The First Corporate Rights Claims

As corporations grew larger and more powerful in the 1830s and 1840s, they began testing the boundaries of state regulation. Could they claim constitutional protections? Could they escape state oversight?

The answer, initially, was "no" to both questions.

In *The Trustees of Dartmouth College v. Woodward* (1819), the Supreme Court ruled that a corporate charter was a contract that states couldn't just arbitrarily revoke; there had to be cause. This gave corporations "artificial personhood" capabilities and some stability, but it didn't make them persons with constitutional rights.

Chief Justice John Marshall, writing for the Court in that case, emphasized that corporations are merely "artificial beings, invisible, intangible, and existing only in contemplation of law." They possessed only those properties that their charter granted them by the state in which they were incorporated.

That early decision protected contract rights, not corporate constitutional rights.

Through the 1830s and 1840s, corporations (mostly railroads, but also banks and trading companies) brought case after case claiming they deserved the same constitutional protections as human beings. They lost consistently. Courts understood the difference between natural persons and artificial legal entities.

The Civil War Changes Everything

The Civil War transformed America's economy. Prior to 1860, most corporations were small, local, and tightly regulated. After 1865, massive national corporations emerged in part because of federal subsidies, especially the railroads to which Lincoln had given tens of millions of acres of federal lands.

These new national railroads weren't like earlier corporations. They operated across state lines, employed thousands, and controlled vast wealth. And they had every incentive to escape state regulation as a way of jacking up their profits.

The Fourteenth Amendment, ratified in 1868, gave them the opening they'd been searching for.

The Amendment's framers never mentioned corporations. The congressional debates around it focused exclusively on protecting the recently freed slaves. Every speech, every argument, every explanation we can find on the record concerned racial equality and civil rights for Black Americans.

But the amendment used the word "person" rather than "natural person" or "citizen." And that got the corporate lawyers' attention.

The Fourteenth Amendment Campaign

Starting in 1868, corporations launched a systematic campaign to claim Fourteenth Amendment rights as railroad after railroad brought cases arguing that state regulation violated their rights as "persons" under the amendment.

In *The Railroad Tax Cases* (1872), which Stephen Field had brought to the Court from the 9th Circuit, the railroad corporations argued that "discriminatory taxation" violated their Fourteenth Amendment rights. They (and Field) lost.

In *Munn v. Illinois* (1877), grain warehouse companies (with Field's agreement) argued that state regulation of their rates violated their Fourteenth Amendment rights to the sanctity of property. They also lost.

Chief Justice Morrison Waite, writing for the majority in *Munn*, firmly rejected corporate constitutional rights: "When private property is devoted to a public use, it is subject to public regulation."

The Court consistently ruled that the Fourteenth Amendment was meant to protect the recently freed enslaved people, not big corporations. Regulation of corporate activity for the public good was entirely constitutional.

But the corporations kept trying. They had, after all, virtually unlimited legal budgets so they could afford to lose ninety-nine cases if they won the hundredth. And they knew that the composition of the Court changed over time and may one day become more amenable to their arguments.

What the Oligarchs Were Fighting Against

To understand why corporations fought so hard for constitutional rights, you first have to realize what they were frantically fighting against: the First Progressive Era and everything it promised to working-class people.

By the 1870s and 1880s, democratic grass-roots movements were challenging corporate power across America. States were responding with laws that would have seemed impossibly radical just a generation earlier, limiting both corporate activity and money in politics.

The income tax was being debated repeatedly during that era, and would eventually become the Sixteenth Amendment in 1913, giving the federal government the ability to tax corporations as well as individuals and fund public infrastructure and benefits. (Prior to that, most federal funding came from tariffs.) Corporate lawyers fought the income tax relentlessly, arguing that it violated corporate property rights.

Direct election of senators was also being demanded back then; they used to be appointed by the states. State legislatures, however, had been notoriously corrupt, with corporate money buying Senate seats, leading to multiple bribery scandals (the most notorious was in Montana in 1899). The Seventeenth Amendment in 1913 would give that power to voters instead. Corporate interests fought it right to the bitter end, because they'd largely perfected the dark art of bribing state legislators.

Labor protections were also spreading nationwide. States were limiting working hours, requiring safety standards, and prohibiting child labor. Corporate lawyers fought every one of these laws, unsuccessfully claiming they constituted unconstitutional interference with property rights and freedom of contract.

In response to national outrage about the growing concentrations of wealth at the top of the corporate world, antitrust laws were being proposed. The Sherman Antitrust Act would pass in 1890, giving the federal government the power to break up monopolies. Corporate lawyers spent the next century trying to gut it before five corrupt Republicans on the Supreme Court helped them out in the twentieth century.[23]

In short, corporations were battling virtually everything that would later build the American Dream: every protection for workers, every tax on wealth, and every regulation of corporate behavior. They opposed, in other words, pretty much any and all democratic reforms that threatened their oligarchic power.

But they needed constitutional weapons to fight back if they wanted to be able to rise above state laws and regulations; and corporate constitutional rights, turning on the Fourteenth Amendment, would give them exactly that.

Roscoe Conkling's Conspiracy Theory

In 1882, a curious event occurred that would later fuel claims about the Fourteenth Amendment's "true" purpose that last to this day.

Roscoe Conkling, a former US senator who'd served on the joint committee that drafted the Fourteenth Amendment, appeared as a witness on behalf of the railroads before the Supreme Court in the 1885 *San Mateo County v. Southern Pacific Railroad Company* case, another Stephen Field decision in the 9th Circuit that came before the Supreme Court with an "equal protection" argument. Conkling was now a high-priced corporate lawyer, and the railroad paid him handsomely to testify.

Conkling presented what he claimed was a "secret journal" from the joint committee's congressional deliberations. This supposed journal, Conkling argued, proved that the committee had intentionally used the word "person" instead of "citizen" or "natural person" to specifically include corporations.

It was a lie.

No such secret journal existed. Conkling had manipulated a handful of notes from the deliberations to make it appear the committee had discussed corporate rights. But later historians found the committee's actual debates, thoroughly documented in the public record, and those discussions focused *exclusively* on protecting freed slaves.

Conkling's "conspiracy theory" brazenly further claimed that the Fourteenth Amendment's framers had secretly intended to protect corporations but pretended it was about racial equality just to get it passed.

This was also nonsense. The framers of the amendment discussed their intentions publicly and repeatedly; there was no secret corporate protection agenda.

But Conkling's argument gave that era's corporate lawyers the talking point they needed. Even though the Supreme Court didn't decide *San*

Mateo on constitutional grounds, Conkling's conspiracy theory persisted. Some corporate attorneys still argue it today.

The Pattern of Defeat

Through the 1870s and into the early 1880s, corporations fought and lost case after case claiming Fourteenth Amendment rights:

† *Munn v. Illinois* (1877): Lost. States can regulate businesses affected with a public interest.

† *Railroad Commission Cases* (1886, decided just before *Santa Clara*): Lost. States can regulate railroad rates.

† *Stone v. Farmers' Loan & Trust Co.* (1886): Lost on the constitutional question, though they won on other grounds.

The pattern was clear. The Supreme Court justices (other than Field) weren't buying the corporate lawyers' constitutional rights arguments. The Fourteenth Amendment meant what its framers said it meant: protection for freed slaves, not protection for soulless corporations that were mere creations of state law.

Corporate lawyers determined they needed a different strategy, as they couldn't win by honest argument. So, they stopped trying to win that way and went straight to the Court's reporter, J.C. Bancroft Davis.

The *Santa Clara* End Run

The genius of the *Santa Clara* headnote strategy, if you can call fraud genius, was its indirection.

The railroad didn't need to win on the constitutional question: they just needed to get inserted into the official record that the chief justice claimed the Court had already decided the question.

J.C. Bancroft Davis's headnote accomplished this perfectly. Future courts would cite *Santa Clara*'s headnote without ever reading the actual decision. They'd rely on Davis's summary, which fraudulently claimed the Court had ruled on corporate constitutional rights.

The seventy-year legal war for corporate rights ended not with a victory in court but a sleight of hand in the court reporter's office.

After 1886, the record shows, corporations stopped losing Fourteenth Amendment cases because courts now cited the *Santa Clara* headnote as establishing that corporations were persons. The precedent was manufactured by Davis, of course, but it became precedent nonetheless the first time another decision cited it.

That first happened in 1889, in *Minneapolis & St. Louis Railway Company v. Beckwith*, when the Supreme Court itself cited the *Santa Clara* headnote in ruling for corporate constitutional rights without questioning whether the earlier case had actually decided that issue.

The lie had become the law. The seventy-year war was over. The corporations had won.

Not through honest argument. Not through democratic process. Through fraud.

The Progressive Era Fights Back

Corporate constitutional rights didn't stop the First Progressive Era: it just made the fight a hell of a lot harder.

Between 1890 and 1920, reformers won remarkable victories despite these repeated corporate constitutional claims. The Sherman Antitrust Act passed in 1890. The income tax became constitutional through the Sixteenth Amendment in 1913. Direct election of senators came through the Seventeenth Amendment in 1913. Women won the right to vote through the Nineteenth Amendment in 1920.

Over shrieks of outrage from corporate lawyers, states passed worker protections, food safety laws, and regulations on corporate behavior, particularly with regard to their participation in politics.

Muckraking journalists gleefully exposed corporate abuses, outraging working people. Teddy Roosevelt busted trusts (monopolies) to the delight of small businesses. Woodrow Wilson created the Federal Reserve and the Federal Trade Commission to take control of the economy away from private banks and corporations and give it both stability and credibility.

But at every step, corporate lawyers used their new constitutional rights defined in the *Santa Clara* headnote to fight back. They challenged the income tax as a taking of property. They challenged hundreds of labor laws as violations of freedom of contract. They challenged antitrust enforcement as interference with corporate due process rights.

Sometimes they even won. In *Lochner v. New York* (1905), the Supreme Court struck down a state law limiting bakers to working sixty hours per week, ruling that the law violated the "liberty of contract" protected by the Fourteenth Amendment.

The Lochner Era, as it came to be called, saw both state and federal courts successfully and repeatedly striking down progressive legislation for decades—minimum wage laws, maximum hour laws, child labor restrictions, worker safety requirements. All were challenged as violations of the corporate Fourteenth Amendment constitutional rights allegedly granted by *Santa Clara,* and the Court went along with the corporate lawyers in nearly every case.

The fraudulent headnote of 1886 had given corporations a weapon they would use against every democratic reform for generations, including right up to this very day.

The Seeds of the Second Progressive Era

The First Progressive Era, however, laid the groundwork for something even bigger. Despite corporate resistance, it established a set of core principles that would again flower in the 1930s with President Franklin D. Roosevelt's New Deal.

The income tax created a mechanism to fund public goods and redistribute wealth. The direct election of senators made the federal government more accountable to voters. Antitrust laws established the principle that corporate power could be constrained by government. And labor protections, though often struck down by courts (including to this day), established the principle that workers had at least some rights.

When the Republican Great Depression hit in 1929 and FDR was elected to solve the problem in 1932, these foundations were ready. Franklin Roosevelt built on them to create the New Deal, launching a Second

Progressive Era that would finally make the American Dream real for a majority of Americans, at least until Reagan and the GOP took a meat axe to it.

But corporate constitutional rights remained, as the fraudulent precedent of *Santa Clara* was never overturned or, frankly, even carefully examined. It sat in constitutional law like a dormant virus, waiting for the right conditions to reactivate.

Those conditions came in 1981, when Ronald Reagan took office and began the systematic dismantling of almost everything the Progressive Eras had built.

To clearly see how we got from 1886 to today, we first must know what the Founders actually believed about corporations. Their vision, it turns out, was the polar opposite of corporate constitutional rights. And recovering that vision is essential to undoing Davis's and Field's crime.

6

The First Corporate War

Every american schoolchild learns about the boston tea Party, and most also learn it was about "taxation without representation."

That's true, but hugely incomplete.

The Boston Tea Party was, in reality, fundamentally a rebellion against raw corporate power. The tea being dumped belonged to the British East India Company, then the world's largest corporate monopoly. The tyranny being resisted was a new form of corporate tyranny corruptly backed by Company stockholder King George III's government force.

The Founders of this nation, then, fought a revolution every bit as much against a corporation as against the British military. Understanding this history explains why they would've been horrified by the idea of corporate constitutional rights.

The Company That Ruled the World

The British East India Company was not like modern corporations: it was also, essentially, a private army with a corporate charter—a state unto itself.

It had its own military, its own courts, its own laws. It conquered nations, ruled hundreds of millions of people via its own appointed governors, and extracted wealth on a scale that dwarfed the British government itself.

By the 1770s, the Company controlled most of India, ran the opium trade into China, and dominated global commerce, including North

America. It was more powerful than most governments. It could—and did—wage wars, negotiate treaties, and legally execute prisoners. It answered to stockholders, the King, and his Parliament, not average citizens or voters.

The Company's stockholders included members of Parliament, British aristocrats, and the King himself. These conflicts of interest meant Company interests heavily shaped eighteenth-century British policy. When the Company wanted something, Parliament often gave it.

The Company was the original too-big-to-fail corporation. When it faced bankruptcy in 1773, Parliament bailed it out by granting it a monopoly on tea sales in the American colonies, thus outlawing the now-illegal importation of tea by independent merchants and traders.

That was the Tea Act of 1773, which American colonists correctly understood as corporate tyranny enforced by government power.

A Voice from the Revolution

I searched for years to find a firsthand account of what actually happened in Boston Harbor that cold December night in 1773. The participants in the Tea Party were sworn to secrecy for fifty years, by which time most were dead, so most of what they thought and felt was lost to history.

Then, in an antique bookstore in London, I found a treasure. It was sitting on a shelf with a bunch of old books from the early nineteenth century, a part of the store that smelled of dust, wax, and aging paper. When I saw it, I was astonished: I'd been looking for something like it for decades.

I immediately purchased an original copy of *Retrospect of the Boston Tea Party with a Memoir of George R.T. Hewes, a Survivor of the Little Band of Patriots Who Drowned the Tea in Boston Harbour in 1773*, published in New York by S.S. Bliss in 1834.

The book's author, James Hawkes, interviewed George Robert Twelvetrees Hewes, who was a shoemaker and a patriot. He knew Samuel Adams and John Hancock personally. He was present at the Boston Massacre. And on the night of December 16, 1773, he was one of the men who boarded the Company's ships.

Hawkes's interview of Hewes, published sixty-one years after the event, is the only actual first-person account in existence of the Boston Tea Party by a participant.

Most significantly, what Hewes described to Hawkes in this little book wasn't just a tax revolt: it was an explicit rebellion against corporate power.

The Corporate Monopoly

Many people today think the Tea Act of 1773 simply raised taxes on tea. It did not: it was actually a massive tax cut.

The purpose of the Tea Act was to give the East India Company full and unlimited access to the American tea trade so it could sell the surplus tea it had built up in its warehouses over the previous three years during a pretty severe recession.

It exempted the Company from having to pay taxes to Britain on that tea exported to the colonies, and even gave the Company a tax refund on the millions of pounds of tea it was holding in inventory.

Because the Company no longer had to pay high taxes to England and held a monopoly on colonial tea sales, it could lower its prices to undercut local importers and the mom-and-pop tea merchants in every town in America. Additionally, it allowed the British navy to intercept tea "smugglers" to the colonies, seize their ships and cargo, and imprison their crews.

It wasn't "taxation without representation": it was "tax breaks for giant corporations without representation" and a government-granted monopoly.

This was what specifically infuriated the colonists. They resented their colonies being used as a profit center for a multinational corporation and their small businesses no longer being able to buy tea from "pirates" (private ships bringing tea to the colonies) because the Company had an exclusive, monopolistic right of sale in North America.

"Taxation without representation" meant something specific to that generation: hitting the average person and small business with taxes while giving the most powerful corporation in the world one of the most massive tax breaks in history. It was government sponsorship of one corporation over all competitors, plain and simple.

According to Hewes, colonists were either boycotting Company tea or buying smuggled tea to avoid supporting the Company's profits. This resistance, he said, had "greatly diminished the importation into the colonies of this commodity."

Meanwhile, he noted, "an immense quantity of it was accumulated in the warehouses of the East India Company in England. This company petitioned the King to suppress the duty of three pence per pound upon its introduction into America."

The King granted the petition with the Tea Act, and the Company's ships set sail for America with their monopoly tea.

The Alarm Goes Out

A newsletter called *The Alarm* circulated through the colonies. One issue, signed by the enigmatic "Rusticus," made clear the feelings of colonial Americans about England's largest corporation:

> Are we in like Manner to be given up to the Disposal of the East India Company, who have now the Assurance, to step forth in Aid of the Minister, to execute his Plan, of enslaving America? Their Conduct in Asia, for some Years past, has given simple Proof, how little they regard the Laws of Nations, the Rights, Liberties, or Lives of Men. They have levied War, excited Rebellions, dethroned lawful Princes, and sacrificed Millions for the Sake of Gain.
>
> The Revenues of Mighty Kingdoms have centered in their Coffers. And these not being sufficient to glut their Avarice, they have, by the most unparalleled Barbarities, Extortions, and Monopolies, stripped the miserable Inhabitants of their Property, and reduced whole Provinces to Indigence and Ruin. Fifteen hundred Thousands, it is said, perished by Famine in one Year, not because the Earth denied its Fruits; but because this Company and their Servants engulfed all the Necessaries of Life, and set them at so high a Rate that the poor could not purchase them.

One and a half million people died, Rusticus wrote, in a single year, not from natural disasters but from corporate greed.

The colonists knew exactly what kind of monster they were facing. They'd seen what the East India Company did to India and were determined it wouldn't happen to their America.

Another pamphlet, signed "Hampden," declared: "It hath now been proved to you that the East India Company obtained the monopoly of that trade by bribery and corruption. That the power thus obtained they have prostituted to extortion, and other the most cruel and horrible purposes, the sun ever beheld."

Philadelphia and New York Resist

The battle began in Philadelphia.

According to Hewes, "those to whom the teas of the Company were intended to be consigned, were induced by persuasion, or constrained by menaces, to promise, on no terms, to accept the proffered consignment."

In New York, Captains Sears and McDougal, "daring and enterprising men, effected a concert of will between the smugglers, the merchants, and the sons of liberty." The small businessmen, the entrepreneurs, and the patriots had joined forces. In many cases, like Paul Revere and Sam Adams, they were the same people.

"Pamphlets suited to the conjecture, were daily distributed," Hewes affirmed, "and nothing was left unattempted by popular leaders, to obtain their purpose."

The Company's ships were turned back from Philadelphia and New York. The colonists had drawn a line.

Then the ships arrived in Boston.

The Decisive Moment

"On the twenty-eighth of November, 1773," Hewes told Hawkes, "the ship *Dartmouth* with 112 chests arrived; and the next morning after, the following notice was widely circulated: 'Friends, Brethren, Countrymen! That worst of plagues, the detested TEA, has arrived in this harbor. The hour of destruction, a manly opposition to the machinations of tyranny, stares you in the face. Every friend to his country, to himself, and to posterity, is now called upon to meet in Faneuil Hall, at nine o'clock, this day, at which time the bells will ring, to make a united and successful resistance to this last, worst, and most destructive measure of administration.'"

The colonists gathered. The Company's local agents were urged to renounce their positions, but they refused and instead took refuge in a nearby British fortress.

A guard was placed on Griffin's Wharf, near where the tea ships were moored. Messengers stood ready to ride to neighboring towns if the Company made any moves.

Hewes recalls the voices of the Bostonians during a hastily convened meeting in a local pub: "Why do we wait? Soon or late we must engage in conflict with England. The opposition is formed; it is general; it remains for us to seize the occasion. The more we delay the more strength is acquired by the [British] ministers. Now is the time to prove our courage."

A local tea seller named Rotch was asked to demand that the Governor permit the ships to return to England. The Governor refused, citing the honor of the laws and duty toward the King.

The meeting erupted. A man disguised as an Indian shouted from the gallery. The crowd dissolved in an instant and rushed to Griffin's Wharf.

The Tea Party had begun.

That Night in the Harbor

Hewes was there. His account is vivid:

> It was now evening, and I immediately dressed myself in the costume of an Indian, equipped with a small hatchet, which I and my associates denominated the tomahawk, with which, and a club, after having painted my face and hands with coal dust in the shop of a blacksmith, I repaired to Griffin's wharf, where the ships lay that contained the tea.
>
> When I first appeared in the street after being thus disguised, I fell in with many who were dressed, equipped and painted as I was, and who fell in with me and marched in order to the place of our destination.

Between one hundred and one hundred and fifty men gathered at the wharf. They were divided into three parties, one for each ship, and Hewes was appointed boatswain of his group and sent to demand the keys to the hatches from the ship's captain.

"I made the demand accordingly," he said, "and the captain promptly replied, and delivered the articles; but requested me at the same time to do no damage to the ship or rigging."

The captain of a Company ship stood by and watched as the colonists destroyed the Company's property. He asked only that they not damage the ship itself. He knew which way the wind was blowing. Hewes continued:

> We then were ordered by our commander to open the hatches and take out all the chests of tea and throw them overboard, and we immediately proceeded to execute his orders, first cutting and splitting the chests with our tomahawks, so as thoroughly to expose them to the effects of the water. In about three hours from the time we went on board, we had thus broken and thrown overboard every tea chest to be found in the ship, while those in the other ships were disposing of the tea in the same way, at the same time. We were surrounded by British armed ships, but no attempt was made to resist us.

Three hundred forty-two chests. Over ninety thousand pounds of tea. Enough to make twenty-four million cups. Worth over two million dollars in today's money.

All of it destroyed to make a point about corporate power.

No Tea Shall Survive

The participants were absolutely committed that none of the East India Company's tea would ever be consumed on American shores. Hewes describes what happened to those who tried to pocket some for themselves:

> During the time we were throwing the tea overboard, there were several attempts made by some of the citizens of Boston and its vicinity to carry off small quantities of it for their family use. To effect that object, they would watch their opportunity to snatch up a handful from the deck, where it became plentifully scattered, and put it into their pockets.
>
> One Captain O'Conner, whom I well knew, came on board for that purpose, and when he supposed he was not noticed, filled his pockets, and also the lining of his coat. But I had detected him and gave information to the captain of what he was doing. We were ordered to take him into custody, and just as he was stepping from the vessel, I seized him by the skirt of his coat, and in attempting to pull him back, I tore it off; but, springing forward, by a rapid effort he made his escape. He had, however, to run a gauntlet through the crowd upon the wharf; each one, as he passed, giving him a kick or a stroke.

An old man with a large cocked hat and white wig slipped some tea into his pocket. They caught him, threw his hat and wig into the harbor along with the tea, and let him escape with "now and then a slight kick."

The next morning, considerable quantities of tea were found floating on the water. Small boats rowed out and beat it with oars and paddles until it was thoroughly destroyed.

"We then quietly retired to our several places of residence," Hewes concludes, "without having any conversation with each other, or taking any measures to discover who were our associates.... There appeared to be an understanding that each individual should volunteer his services, keep his own secret, and risk the consequence for himself. No disorder took place during that transaction, and it was observed at that time that the stillest night ensued that Boston had enjoyed for many months."

The War Begins

The British Parliament responded immediately.

The Boston Port Act closed the port of Boston until the citizens reimbursed the East India Company for the tea they'd destroyed.

The colonists refused.

A year and a half later, on April 19, 1775, the colonists would again defy the Company and Great Britain, this time taking on British troops in armed conflict at Lexington and Concord, the "shots heard 'round the world."

That war, triggered by a transnational corporation and its government's patrons trying to deny American colonists a fair and competitive marketplace, would last until 1783.

The Declaration of Independence, written in 1776, lists the colonies' grievances against King George III and specifically mentions taxes, troops, judges, and governors.

It never mentions the East India Company by name, but it didn't have to. Everyone understood. The King's tyranny and the Company's tyranny were the same tyranny. The Company had bought the government, so fighting the King meant fighting corporate power.

The Lesson the Founders Learned

The men who wrote the Constitution had fought a corporation. They'd seen what unchecked corporate power could do. They'd watched the East India Company starve millions in India, corrupt Parliament, and try to monopolize American commerce.

And they were determined it would never happen here again.

The US Constitution contains about 4,400 words. It establishes the structure of government, enumerates powers, and limits authority.

But it never mentions corporations. Not once.

This was not an oversight. The Founders knew about corporations. They had fought one. They deliberately chose not to give corporations constitutional status or protection.

Corporations were creatures of state law, to be kept on a short leash by state legislatures close to the people. They could be chartered, regulated, and dissolved by the states and, at our country's founding, had no rights whatsoever under the federal Constitution.

The American antipathy toward the East India Company continued even after the Revolution. When the Company tried to resume postwar trading with America, offering clothing, silks, coffee, and spices, the Americans refused. The trade war continued to and through the War of 1812.

The Founders had not forgotten. And they made sure corporate power would never gain the same foothold in America that it had held in the colonies.

Or so they thought.

A century later, a court reporter and a corrupt justice would undo much of their work with a few strokes of a pen.

7

What the Founders Knew

T HE COLONISTS WHO FOUGHT THE AMERICAN REVOLUTION AND wrote our Constitution knew well who and what were the most dangerous enemies of democracy. It wasn't just King George III; it was his British East India Company, the most powerful corporation in the world.

This is why the Constitution never mentions corporations and why our nation's Founders would have been horrified by corporate constitutional rights. Instead of a nation ruled by oligarchs and their businesses, the Founders and Framers of the Constitution envisioned a nation of independent citizens, small farmers, entrepreneurs, and journeymen who owned the fruit of their labor and enjoyed a continually improving standard of living.

Although Hamilton's vision was more industrial and Jefferson's more agrarian, both saw a future for our nation, in their own ways, that we today call the American Dream.

The Supreme Court–created doctrine of corporate constitutional rights, however, is the opposite of our Founders' vision. It now dominates America through economic, political, and legal mechanisms that allow a small, wealthy group of oligarchs to dominate the rest of us. Our Founders fought a revolution to stop—and, moving forward, prevent—exactly that.

The Founders' Vision of Economic Fredom

The Founders didn't just fight the Revolutionary War to seize political freedom from the British Crown as it says in most of the history books our kids read; they also wanted economic freedom from the East India Company. They wanted a nation where We the People made the decisions, rather than having them imposed on us by billionaire tech bros and giant corporations.

Thomas Jefferson explicitly wanted a nation of independent yeoman farmers, each owning enough land to support a family, with only a very few dependent on wages from a wealthy employer. This vision was small-d democratic to its core: citizens who owned their own means of livelihood couldn't be controlled by employers or landlords. With the rights enumerated in the Bill of Rights, they could vote their consciences, speak their minds, and participate in self-governance as political equals.

Benjamin Franklin, who rose from a penniless apprentice to become one of the most successful businessmen in the colonies, embodied the promise that hard work and talent could lift anyone to prosperity, even in the early republic. His story was the original American Dream, long before that phrase even existed.

This vision of a new, free America required government to limit corporate power. If, like the East India Company, corporations could grow without limit, accumulate mind-boggling levels of wealth, and use that financial power to buy influence with politicians and thus government, they'd essentially recreate the very tyranny the Founders fought the Revolution to overthrow.

Franklin himself warned about what we today call oligarchy (aka rule by the morbidly rich). "Only a virtuous people are capable of freedom," he wrote. "As nations become corrupt and vicious, they have more need of masters."

Two centuries later, Franklin Roosevelt would echo his namesake Ben Franklin's insight when he famously declared in 1936 that "necessitous men are not free men." Both of these two men who transformed America understood that economic security was the necessary foundation of political freedom. And they both knew corporate and oligarchic control of our economy and our politics threatened to destroy both.

The Declaration's Missing Word

The Founders weren't just starry-eyed believers in democracy; they were also strategic. They framed the American Revolution as a fight for "natural rights" against monarchical tyranny, using a message that played very well in Enlightenment-era Europe (particularly in pre-revolutionary France), where they needed support.

Explicitly calling out the world's most powerful corporation in the Declaration might have complicated things, so the Founders tried to make sure corporate power would never gain the same foothold in America as it had in Britain, India, and other places across the world that were groaning under the Company's yoke.

The Constitution's Silence

In addition to establishing the structure of our government, our Constitution also (following Montesquieu's advice) divides power among three branches, and limits the authority of each branch.

But even with all that, the Constitution never mentions corporations. Not even once.

This was *not* an oversight. The Founders knew all about corporations; after all, they'd fought one to establish this nation. Which is why they deliberately chose not to give corporations constitutional status or any sorts of protection whatsoever.

James Madison, Alexander Hamilton, and others understood that corporations were useful tools for specific purposes: building a canal, establishing a bank, constructing roads and other essential infrastructure. But they were only tools to be regulated by We the People through our elected representatives, not autonomous entities with their own rights.

The Constitution grants Congress the power to regulate commerce. It gives states responsibility for chartering corporations. But it doesn't grant corporations *any* rights whatsoever.

James Madison wrote to his mentor, Thomas Jefferson, on October 24, 1787 (just weeks after they'd finished writing the Constitution), about his concern for possible future corruption by "the representatives of Counties and Corporations in the Legislatures of the States much more disposed to sacrifice the aggregate interest, and even authority...over the interests of the nation."

But, because the power to bring corporations into existence and regulate their behavior was left by the Constitution entirely to the states, he didn't believe America would ever again have to confront a giant monopoly like the East India Company.

"Many illustrations might be given of this impossibility," he wrote. "How long has it taken to fix, and how imperfectly is yet fixed, the legislative power of corporations, though that power is subordinate in the most compleat manner? The line of distinction between the power of regulating trade and that of drawing revenue from it, which was once considered the barrier of our liberties [by the King and the Company], was found on fair discussion, to be absolutely undefinable."

When the Bill of Rights was added to the Constitution in 1791, it explicitly protected *human* rights: speech, religion, assembly, due process, and trial by jury. These were what the Founders considered "natural rights" given to us by what the Declaration of Independence calls "Nature's God" to human beings, not artificial privileges for legal fictions called corporations.

The Founders would have ridiculed—or been horrified by—the idea that a corporation, a piece of paper, a legal abstraction, could ever achieve the same rights as human beings.

Jefferson's Warning

Thomas Jefferson never stopped worrying about corporate power. In letter after letter, he warned about the danger of "moneyed corporations" becoming a new aristocracy.

In 1816, Jefferson wrote: "I hope we shall crush in its birth the aristocracy of our moneyed corporations, which dare already to challenge our government to a trial of strength and bid defiance to the laws of our country."

Jefferson saw it coming, though, during the 1820s, after his presidency, as the country experienced explosive growth and the first steam-powered railroads emerged. Banks, manufacturing corporations, southern plantations, and the New York trading companies were accumulating dangerous levels of power. They were buying politicians, manipulating markets, and acting as if they were above democratic control.

Jefferson's solution was strict regulation and charter revocation for corporations that violated the public interest. Like every other one of the Founders, he never once suggested corporations should have the constitutional rights he and his peers had put their lives on the line for; that would have seemed insane to him.

Jefferson and his peers understood something that over a century of corporate constitutional rights has caused us to forget: corporations exist solely at the pleasure of the people acting through state governments. We create them. We can constrain them. We can destroy them. They have no inherent right to exist, just the privileges that we grant them.

Madison's Insights

James Madison, who drafted much of the Constitution, also understood the danger of concentrated economic power, particularly when it was combined with political influence.

In *Federalist No. 10*, Madison warned about "factions," groups he defined as having interests "adversed to the rights of other citizens, or to the permanent and aggregate interests of the community." He and his colleagues in the Convention of 1787 designed the Constitution's checks and balances explicitly to prevent any single faction from dominating our government.

But Madison could barely have imagined corporations as large as modern multinationals. The biggest corporations in 1788 America were tiny compared to the British East India Company, which Madison and the others had seen as a dangerous aberration worth fighting a war against, not a model for the future of their new republic.

Madison's design of the Constitution assumed that economic power would be relatively dispersed and that governments would control corporations, not the other way around.

Corporate constitutional rights, established in the late 1880s, however, reversed this. Instead of government controlling corporations, a corrupt Supreme Court justice and his court reporter henchman gave corporations the constitutional weapons they'd eventually use to fight virtually any semblance of government control.

The Early State Experience

The first American states took seriously their power to control corporations. In the early republic, state legislatures granted corporate charters sparingly and with extraordinarily strict conditions. Corporate charters were required to specify the purpose of the corporation, and it couldn't do anything else. They specified how long the corporation could exist, typically twenty to thirty years (none were established in perpetuity). They defined how much capital a company could control, where it could operate, what it could own, who could serve as directors, and what reports it had to file.

Throughout the nineteenth century, state legislatures regularly revoked charters of corporations that violated their terms or acted against the public interest. The corporate death sentence was a real possibility and was frequently invoked.

In the minds of these early politicians, this wasn't anti-business: it was a new American democracy controlling its own artificial-person creations.

Pennsylvania, Ohio, and other states revoked dozens of corporate charters in the 1800s for various offenses: failure to serve the public interest, corruption, violation of charter terms, or simply because the legislature decided the corporation was no longer needed.

Corporations were simply viewed as tools of commerce, and when a tool broke or became dangerous, you threw it away.[24]

What Changed

Two things destroyed this system of state-level democratic corporate control.

First, after the Civil War, states began competing for the revenue that could be had from corporate charter fees, employment, and taxes on business activities. In response to a challenge to Ohio's corporate antitrust laws by John D. Rockefeller's Standard Oil Trust, New Jersey pioneered "charter mongering," offering weak regulations and low taxes to attract corporate charters. Other states followed (including Delaware, where more than half of American corporations are today chartered), and a race to the bottom began during what's today referred to as the "Chartermongering Era."

Second, the adoption of the *Santa Clara* headnote by the Supreme Court in the 1890s gave corporations constitutional rights that made state control much harder. Once corporations could claim due process, equal protection, privacy, free speech, and other constitutional rights, revoking charters became legally complex and, with the largest corporations, extraordinarily expensive.

The combination proved deadly to democracy. Weak state regulations plus corporate constitutional rights brought late nineteenth-century America corporate power and the rise of dynastic wealth, all without democratic accountability.

The Founders had designed a system to prevent exactly this outcome, but Davis's and Field's corporate constitutional rights destroyed it.

From the Founders to FDR

The Founders' vision of economic freedom, of citizens owning their own labor and controlling their own destinies, didn't die with corporate constitutional rights in the 1890s. It went underground, waiting for the right moment to reemerge.

That moment came in 1933, when President Franklin D. Roosevelt took office in the depths of the Republican Great Depression.

FDR understood what the Founders both knew and proclaimed: that economic security is the foundation of political freedom. "Necessitous men are not free men," he repeatedly declared. People who are hungry, out of a job, or who can't afford a doctor or a home, are not truly free, he said, no matter what rights the Constitution guarantees them on paper.

Roosevelt built on the Founders' vision to create the American Dream in its modern form with a massive collection of nation-changing laws and government agencies he called The New Deal. They included the right to a job that paid a living wage, the right to organize and bargain collectively, the right to a secure retirement, and the right to access a basic social safety net that kept job losses or natural disasters from destroying families.

By 1981, that vision had become reality for two-thirds of American families. A single income could support a family, and you could buy a house for three times your annual salary. College was affordable, even with a part-time job (as I experienced). Healthcare didn't bankrupt people, and, with Social Security and Medicare, retirement was finally secure.

Most of the Founders would have lauded this new America that FDR brought about and LBJ fine-tuned. Over loud Republican objections to the right to unionize, the minimum wage, Social Security, and pretty much every other New Deal and Great Society program, we finally became the nation of independent, economically secure citizens they'd envisioned, updated for the industrial age.

But corporate constitutional rights remained embedded in the law, a time bomb planted in 1886. Thus, when Ronald Reagan activated it in 1981, the American Dream began to die.[25]

Recovering the Founders' Vision

The Founders got it right: Corporations can be useful tools, but they must be controlled by democratic governance for the benefit of society as well as their wealthy owners. They'd have no inherent rights, only granted privileges. And when they abused those privileges, they'd be constrained or even destroyed.

The doctrine of corporate constitutional rights Davis and Field kicked off in 1886 turned this vision upside down, giving corporations constitutional weapons first designed exclusively for humans that they could use to fight back efforts at democratic control. It transformed them from servants of the public into our modern-day masters.

Undoing corporate constitutional rights means recovering the Founders' vision, returning corporations to their proper place as *tools* of society, not *rulers* of society. It means restoring the economic freedom and affordability that makes political freedom possible.

It means, in short, rebuilding the American Dream.

But before we can rebuild our nation and our middle class, we first must understand how completely corporate constitutional rights have corrupted our democracy. The story of that corruption reached its climax in 2010, with the Supreme Court's unscrupulous decision by five on-the-take Republicans on the Court in *Citizens United*. That decision, more than any others, shows us what happens when the fraud of 1886 is taken to its logical conclusion.

8

The Crime Pays Off

Davis's fraudulent headnote of 1886 was just the beginning. Over the next 140 years, corporate lawyers would build an empire of constitutional rights on that foundation of fraud. The progression reached its logical conclusion in 2010, when five corrupt Republican Supreme Court justices—several openly on the take from rightwing billionaires and massive corporations—handed morbidly rich oligarchs the power to buy American democracy outright.

Citizens United wasn't just about campaign finance rules or the legalization of bribing Supreme Court justices (although it encompassed both): it was the culmination of a 140-year theft. The oligarchs finally had functionally unlimited constitutional weapons to complete what the southern plantation fascists built prior to the Civil War and the railroad barons started in 1886: the destruction of the American Dream and its replacement with an all-American form of oligarchic feudalism.

The Century of Expansion

Between 1886 and today, corporations have systematically claimed every constitutional right that was written to protect human beings.

First Amendment freedom of free speech? Corporations claimed it in the 1970s and 1980s, arguing they had the right to spend money on political campaigns, advertise tobacco to children, and lie in their marketing.

Second Amendment gun rights? Weapons manufacturing corporations claimed it to challenge state and city laws that protected citizens and schoolchildren from gun violence and to help them market their deadly wares.

Fourth Amendment protections from unreasonable searches and seizures? Corporations claimed it in *Dow Chemical Company v. United States* (1986), arguing the EPA couldn't use aerial photography to detect illegal cancer-causing pollution without a warrant because Dow was a "corporate person."

Fifth Amendment protection against self-incrimination? Corporations claimed it to avoid disclosing evidence of crimes and to conceal the dangers of tobacco (which killed my brother), asbestos (which killed my father), and pesticides (among other things).

I still remember my dad coming home from the tool-and-die shop where he worked, smelling of machine oil, talking over dinner about the Machinists Union and how unions were the reason we had a middle-class life, his discussions with my mom about how they'd travel the world with the pension he was earning. Corporate constitutional rights took that all away from me and my family.

Sixth Amendment right to trial by jury? Corporations demanded it to drag things out and increase the costs to government whenever they were facing regulatory penalties.

Seventh Amendment right to a jury in civil cases? Corporations asserted it while simultaneously forcing consumers and employees into mandatory binding arbitration, denying humans the same right.

Thirteenth Amendment outlawing slavery? Private prison corporations note that the amendment still allows slavery for persons convicted of a crime, so for-profit prison slave labor has become a multibillion-dollar-a-year business that rivals the old Confederacy.

Fourteenth Amendment equal protection and due process? Corporations used these relentlessly to strike down regulations, block taxes, and prevent democratic governance.

The only amendment corporations haven't seriously claimed is the Third (quartering soldiers in private homes), but give them time. Trump, with his increasing militarization of American cities, may still find a way to use it to make money for his billionaire buddies or install ICE agents in our houses and apartment buildings.

Virtually every constitutional right written to protect human dignity, liberty, and democracy has been converted into a weapon for corporate power.

The Destruction of the New Deal

For nearly fifty years, from 1933 to 1980, the American Dream flourished despite Davis's corporate constitutional rights headnote. FDR's New Deal and the regulatory framework that followed it constrained corporate power enough, in fact, to build the largest middle class in world history, the first to exceed half of the nation's population.

The Roosevelt, Truman, Eisenhower, Kennedy, Johnson, Nixon, Ford, and Carter administrations were able to do this because even with corporate constitutional rights on the books, the political will still existed to regulate corporations, tax the wealthy, protect workers, and invest in public goods. The memory of the Republican Great Depression was still fresh. Thanks to FDR, unions were strong. And the courts, while accepting corporate constitutional rights, hadn't yet extended it to its logical extremes.

That all changed with the Republican Reagan Revolution of 1981.

Reagan didn't just cut taxes and deregulate industries: following the advice of the billionaire-funded Heritage Foundation, he activated corporate constitutional rights as weapons against FDR's New Deal framework. His administration and partisans like John Roberts (then a lawyer in Reagan's Justice Department) encouraged corporations to challenge regulations in court, claiming their constitutional rights were being violated. His well-funded judicial appointments put corporate-friendly judges on the bench who would expand corporate rights for decades to come.

The assault on America's democracy and our middle class was systematic. Union busting was justified by corporate property rights. Tax cuts for the wealthy were framed as protecting corporate due process rights. Deregulation was defended as preventing unconstitutional Fifth and Fourteenth Amendment takings of corporate property. Media consolidation was enabled by corporate First Amendment "free speech" claims.

Each piece of the New Deal framework that had built the world's first widespread middle class and the functioning democracy that supported it came under attack. And corporate constitutional rights provided the legal weapons for that attack.

When states tried to protect workers, corporations sued, claiming their contract rights were being violated. When the federal government tried to regulate pollution, corporations claimed unconstitutional Fifth Amendment takings and Fourth Amendment invasions of their privacy. When communities tried to limit corporate political spending, corporations asserted First Amendment free speech protections.

The fraudulent headnote of 1886 had been a hand grenade sitting with its pin intact for decades. Reagan and his successors pulled that pin, and the American Dream began to die so quickly that by 2015 fewer than half of Americans were still in the middle class, and it took two salaries to get there.[26]

But pulling the pin wasn't enough. The oligarchs needed real cover. They needed to make sure that as working families watched their security disappear, they'd blame the wrong people.

Enter the deflection playbook: "welfare queens," "law and order," "illegal immigrants," "taxpayers versus takers." It was a systematic strategy specifically designed to redirect working-class anger away from the morbidly rich and toward the powerless. As I'll detail later in the book, the same oligarchs who destroyed the American Dream became experts at making sure nobody blamed them for it.

The Democratic Tradition of Keeping Corporations out of Politics

For roughly the first half of America's history, states understood that corporations had no business meddling in democratic elections. In 1905, for example, Wisconsin passed a law (Section 4489a, Sec. 1, ch. 492, 1905) that explicitly said: "No corporation doing business in this state shall pay or contribute, or offer, consent or agree to pay or contribute, directly or indirectly, *any* money, property, free service of its officers or employees or thing of value to *any* political party, organization, committee or individual for *any* political purpose whatsoever, or for the purpose of influencing legislation of *any* kind, or to promote or defeat the candidacy of *any* person for nomination, appointment or election to *any* political office" (emphasis added).

Make a special note of those words "*any* political purpose whatsoever."

Wisconsin wasn't hedging or creating loopholes. It was unambiguously saying that corporations have no role messing around in democracy. They don't vote, don't marry, don't get hungry or sick, and can live forever, so they shouldn't be allowed to use their economic power to twist our system of governance to their benefit and to the detriment of We the People.

Wisconsin wasn't alone in those early fights to keep states' democracies free of corporate control; throughout the Progressive Era and beyond, states across America passed similar laws keeping corporate money out of politics. This wasn't even controversial back then; it simply reflected common sense and a widespread distrust of the morbidly rich.

Until five corrupt Republicans on the Supreme Court, armed with Davis's doctrine of corporate constitutional rights, began tearing it down.

The Bellotti Decision

The march toward *Citizens United* really got underway in 1978 with the Supreme Court's *First National Bank of Boston v. Bellotti* decision.

Massachusetts had passed a law prohibiting corporations from spending money to influence ballot initiatives unless the initiative directly affected the corporation's business, arguing that corporate treasuries were so large compared to individual citizens' resources that allowing corporate spending would drown out human/citizens' voices.

Basing their argument on Davis's fraudulent headnote from the 1886 *Santa Clara County* decision, the First National Bank of Boston—whose CEO wanted to put some of the bank's money into a ballot initiative to cut taxes—sued, claiming the bank's First Amendment free speech rights to fund political campaigns were being violated by the law.

As Ciara Torres-Spelliscy noted in 2014:

> In the 1970s, *Santa Clara* was used to justify granting corporations the First Amendment right to spend unlimited corporate funds on ballot initiatives in a case called *Bellotti*. The Court relied on *Santa Clara*'s reading when it stated that "[i]t has been settled for almost a century that corporations are persons within the meaning of the Fourteenth Amendment." Justice Rehnquist, in his dissent, questioned the wisdom of extending corporations political rights: "[T]hose properties, so beneficial in the economic sphere, pose

special dangers in the political sphere." Again, Rehnquist could not convince his brethren.

In *Citizens United*, when the Supreme Court held that political speech is "indispensable to decision making in a democracy, and this is no less true because the speech comes from a corporation," they cited *Bellotti*. Thus, it's only a hop, skip and a jump from *Santa Clara* to *Citizens United*.

In *Sebelius v. Hobby Lobby Stores*, the store chain is claiming that the corporation (and not just its proprietors) has a religious objection to providing certain types of birth control for its workers as required by the Affordable Care Act. Thus, the Court is contemplating expanding corporate constitutional rights to a new logical extreme: First Amendment religious rights. It's no surprise that Hobby Lobby's brief relies on *Bellotti* and *Citizens United*.[27]

The Supreme Court, in the 5–4 *Bellotti* decision, sided with the corporations. Justice Lewis Powell (a Nixon appointee in 1972, a year after he wrote the infamous *Powell Memo*), writing for the majority, held that corporate speech deserved First Amendment protection because "[t]he inherent worth of the speech in terms of its capacity for informing the public does not depend upon the identity of its source."[28]

In other words, it doesn't matter whether speech comes from a human being or a corporation. Speech is speech.

This is absurd on its face: in a democracy, the identity of the speaker exercising First Amendment free speech rights matters enormously. When scientists say cigarettes cause cancer, that's different from when a tobacco corporation says—to protect their profits—that cigarettes are safe.

When citizens go door to door to get signatures for higher taxes to fund schools, that's different from when a corporation showers cash on politicians and judges to oppose those taxes and thus increase profits. When human beings express a political opinion, we're exercising conscience, self-interest, and judgment. When a corporation funds a political opinion by purchasing advertising or showering cash on elected officials, however, it's advancing the financial interests of wealthy shareholders and multimillionaire executives in ways that are often in direct opposition to the public interest.

But Lewis Powell's majority opinion won, and thus—for the first time since FDR's presidency—enshrined the corrupt principle that corporate "speech" (in other words, money, since corporations don't have mouths) has First Amendment protection.

Justice Byron White dissented powerfully in *Bellotti*: "The State has a legitimate interest in regulating corporate participation in political debate in order to prevent corporate domination of the debate and to minimize the use of corporate economic power as a means of distorting the outcome."

White understood what was at stake, but the Republican majority either didn't understand or didn't care.

Bellotti, then, opened the real floodgates that brought Reagan to power two years later and continue to wash over us with corporate cash today. If corporations had First Amendment rights to influence ballot initiatives (*Bellotti*), what about general elections for politicians? What about unlimited spending on electioneering? What about functionally purchasing political outcomes with the vast resources found in corporate coffers?

Those questions would be answered in 2010, with Clarence Thomas—himself the recipient of millions in "gifts" from rightwing billionaires—becoming the deciding vote.

Citizens United: The Oligarchs Strike Back

In the election year of 2008, a rightwing advocacy group called Citizens United produced a political hit piece on Hillary Clinton. They wanted to run it in theaters and as video-on-demand during the 2008 Democratic primary campaign to knock her out of the running.

The Federal Election Commission said the movie violated the Bipartisan Campaign Reform Act of 2002, known as McCain-Feingold, which prohibited corporations from using their general treasury funds for "electioneering communications" within ninety days of an election.

Citizens United sued, arguing their (nonprofit) corporate First Amendment right to free speech was being violated by McCain-Feingold.

The case reached the Supreme Court in 2009, and Citizens United's lawyers first argued narrowly that their specific video should be allowed because the time restrictions were essentially arbitrary.

But the five Republican justices—Roberts, Scalia, Kennedy, Thomas, and Alito—saw an opportunity to do something far bigger: with this single case, they could overturn a century of campaign finance law and give corporations and their morbidly rich oligarch owners the unlimited power to spend money on—and thus influence or even control—elections.

The Republicans on the Court thus asked for re-argument on a much broader question that had never been part of the case in the first place: can the government restrict *any* corporate political spending at all?

As a result, on January 21, 2010, the five Republicans on the Court issued (over the loud objections of the four Democrats) one of the most consequential and destructive decisions in American history.

Justice Anthony Kennedy, writing for the five-justice majority, held that the government cannot restrict independent political expenditures by corporations. Spending money to influence elections is "speech" protected by the First Amendment, he explained, and, under the logic of Davis's headnote, corporations have the same First Amendment rights as human beings.

The Republican justices' reasoning rested entirely on previous cases grounded in *Santa Clara* and its progeny. Corporations are persons. Money is the same thing as speech for a corporation, which otherwise lacks a mouth and vocal cords. Persons have First Amendment rights. Therefore, corporations can spend unlimited money to influence elections.

Kennedy, ignoring the fact that the word *corporation* doesn't appear even once in the Constitution, wrote: "The Government may not suppress political speech on the basis of the speaker's corporate identity," and "The First Amendment does not permit Congress to make these categorical distinctions based on the corporate identity of the speaker."

Justice John Paul Stevens dissented in a ninety-page opinion that dismantled the majority's reasoning piece by piece.

Stevens wrote: "Corporations have no consciences, no beliefs, no feelings, no thoughts, no desires. Corporations help structure and facilitate the activities of human beings, to be sure, and their 'personhood' often serves as a useful legal fiction. But they are not themselves members of 'We the People' by whom and for whom our Constitution was established."

Stevens understood what the majority refused to acknowledge:

corporations are not people, so granting them constitutional rights perverts democracy.

But Stevens was in the four-Democratic-appointee minority, so his dissent had no legal power. The five Republican justices—several clearly on the take themselves at the time—gave the nation's morbidly rich oligarchs exactly what they wanted: the constitutional right to buy elections.

The Immediate Impact

The impact of *Citizens United* was both immediate and catastrophic for democracy and has gotten worse every year since.

In the 2010 midterm elections, the first after *Citizens United*, outside spending by corporations and wealthy individuals more than doubled from the previous midterm. Super PACs, which could accept unlimited corporate money, spent over $300 million. By 2012, outside spending topped $1 billion. By 2020, it exceeded $3 billion, and in 2024 was about $4.5 billion.[29]

So now we can see who were the real "speakers" in these elections: not citizens or even voters. They were almost exclusively wealthy individuals and corporations, many hiding behind layers of anonymity through dark money groups; over 100 billionaire families put over $2.4 billion into the 2024 election alone, with the vast majority going to Trump and the GOP. Corporate PACs kicked in billions more.[30]

Following the logic of Davis's headnote and Lewis Powell's memo, America's oligarchs had been given the keys to corrupt our democracy, and they set about using them with enthusiasm.

The Logical Extension

Thus, it turns out that—predictably—*Citizens United* was just the beginning. Once corporations got their hands on an unlimited First Amendment right to spend money on politics, other corporate rights followed.

In *Burwell v. Hobby Lobby* (2014), the Supreme Court ruled that closely held corporations have religious freedom rights under the Religious

Freedom Restoration Act and the First Amendment. As a result, a non-living soulless corporation could refuse to provide contraception coverage to employees based on its alleged religious beliefs because it was granted religious freedom rights by five corrupt Republicans on the Supreme Court.

Justice Ruth Bader Ginsburg dissented: "In a decision of startling breadth, the Court holds that commercial enterprises, including corporations, along with partnerships and sole proprietorships, can opt out of any law (saving only tax laws) they judge incompatible with their sincerely held religious beliefs."

The five Republican justices, Roberts, Scalia, Kennedy, Thomas, and Alito (the same five from *Citizens United*), nonetheless gave corporations religious rights. When was the last time you saw a corporation kneeling at a church altar?

McCutcheon and the Continuing Assault

In 2014, in *McCutcheon v. Federal Election Commission*, the Supreme Court took this bizarre logic to its next extreme when it struck down aggregate limits on individual campaign contributions. Those same five Republican justices ruled that preventing corruption wasn't enough of a justification to level the political playing field by reining in spending.

Chief Justice Roberts wrote that the First Amendment "is designed and intended to preserve a free and open public discussion of public questions," and—because money is now a stand-in for "speech"—that contribution limits on his, Thomas's, and Alito's morbidly rich patrons infringed this constitutional right to buy politicians and election outcomes.

This is, to use the technical term, *nuts*, but it's now the law. When Elon Musk gave a quarter-billion dollars to Trump and his campaign in 2024, it wasn't "speech" in any meaningful sense. It was an oligarch—the richest man in the world—using his wealth to buy influence, access, and political outcomes that favored his and his companies' bottom lines.

Justice Stephen Breyer dissented, writing: "Where enough money calls the tune, the general public will not be heard," but he was in the minority, so the rest of us are now being drowned out in virtually every election.

The Oligarch Democracy

We now live in what some political scientists call an oligarchic democracy, a system where wealth—both individual and corporate—determines political outcomes more than votes.

The statistics are damning. According to Princeton professor Martin Gilens, who studied 1,800 policy outcomes, because of this bizarre Republican interpretation of the Fourteenth and First Amendments, "economic elites and organized groups representing business interests have substantial independent impacts on US government policy, while average citizens and mass-based interest groups have little or no independent influence."[31]

In other words, what ordinary Americans want has virtually no impact on what policies get enacted. What wealthy elites and corporations want, instead, almost always determines policy outcomes.

Consider all the issues that score well above 60 percent (and often above 80 percent) on national polling: gun control, free or inexpensive college, a national healthcare system, improved public schools, cheap pharmaceuticals, affordable housing, an absolute right to unionize, the right to vote without your name being purged, a meaningful top income tax rate on the rich, getting climate change under control, breaking up monopolies, and equal rights for minorities and women.

None of these things are happening, and it's because big-money interests oppose *all* of them. That isn't democracy; it's an oppressive oligarchy pretending to be a democracy.

And it all traces back to Davis's fraudulent 1886 headnote. Once corporations became "persons" with constitutional rights, this horrible list of outcomes became both predictable and inevitable.

The International Dimension

And these horrors inflicted on us by a series of corrupt Supreme Court decisions and the phony doctrine of corporate constitutional rights they're based on are no longer limited to whacking democracy in our country. America's corporate constitutional rights doctrine has also spread into international law through trade agreements drafted with the "help" of America's largest corporations.

Starting with the Reagan administration, which first negotiated the precursors to NAFTA and the Trans-Pacific Partnership (TPP), multiple bilateral investment treaties now give corporations the right to sue governments in private tribunals whenever government regulations hurt corporate profits. These "investor–state dispute settlement" provisions let corporations trample the will of We the People, and do it in secret.

For example, a Canadian mining company sued El Salvador for refusing to grant a mining permit that El Salvador documented would contaminate its drinking water. A tobacco company sued Uruguay for requiring life-saving health warnings on cigarette packages. An oil company sued Ecuador for regulations protecting its environment.

These aren't really "trade disputes": they're corporations using treaty law—which they gained by financing politicians with their corporate "free speech"—to claim rights superior to democratic governance.

The same logic that gave corporations constitutional rights in America is now giving them treaty rights globally because corporate constitutional rights have gone international.

The world's oligarchs aren't just buying American democracy; they're using our Supreme Court's 5–4 Republican-only decisions to buy sovereignty itself.

The Court That Sold Democracy

The five Republican justices who decided *Citizens United* and *Hobby Lobby*—Roberts, Scalia, Kennedy, Thomas, and Alito—will be remembered by history as the Court that sold American democracy to the world's most toxic and morbidly rich oligarchs.

And they didn't even bother to do it subtly or incrementally. This power grab was done brazenly, overturning a century of precedent to give corporations and their oligarchs functionally unlimited political power.

These five justices claimed to be "originalists" who'd only interpret the Constitution "according to the Founders' intent." But, as history tells us, this nation's Founders would have been horrified by the entire idea of corporate constitutional rights. They quite literally fought a revolution against corporate tyranny and then deliberately excluded corporations from *any* constitutional protections.

As I wrote in *The Hidden History of the Supreme Court and the Betrayal of America*, the "originalism" of the Roberts Court is a fraud, just like the headnote in *Santa Clara*. It's a convenient fiction used to justify the destruction of our democracy.

History will not judge these justices kindly, nor should it. They'll be remembered as the men who murdered American democracy at the request of the very oligarchs who paid to have them appointed.

The American Dream, Murdered

For my father's generation, born during the Republican Great Depression and coming of age with World War II, the American Dream wasn't just a slogan. FDR's massive experiment with Keynesian economics worked; it was a reality for two-thirds of American families by 1980. A single income could support a family. You could buy a house for three times your annual salary. College was affordable or free. Healthcare didn't bankrupt families. Retirement was secure. Children saw better opportunities than their parents.

As mentioned earlier, that reality was built by two Progressive Eras and a series of presidents who worked hard to constrain oligarch and corporate power. The first, from the 1890s through 1920, established the income tax, direct election of senators, women's suffrage, and the first antitrust laws. The second, from 1933 through 1981, created Social Security, the right to organize unions, the minimum wage, and the regulatory framework that prevented corporate abuse.

But today, as we look at the wreckage of the middle class all around us, we can now see that Davis's corporate constitutional rights headnote provided Reagan, the GOP, and their oligarch "donors" with the weapons to tear it all down.

Citizens United was the final blow against our democracy, leading us directly to the Trump presidency. Once corporations and their oligarch owners could spend unlimited money on elections, they could finance politicians who'd cut their taxes, deregulate their industries, crush their workers' unions, and transfer wealth from working families to the oligarchs created by those same companies.

9

The Numbers Don't Lie

Measuring the Death of the Dream

THE DESTRUCTION OF THE AMERICAN DREAM ISN'T JUST AN ABSTRAC-tion; it's measurable. (See Chart 9.1)

In 1980 when Reagan was elected president, at the peak of the American Dream, fully two-thirds of American families were in the middle class. A single income could support a family, buy a house, take an annual vacation, send the kids to college, and even retire with dignity.

Today, only 43 to 47 percent of Americans qualify as middle class (depending on whose numbers and what criteria you use). And it takes two full-time incomes today to achieve what a single union job gave a family in 1980.

Consider wages. If wages had kept pace with productivity since 1980, the median American individual worker's income would be over $100,000 today. Instead, it's around $50,000. With help from the Reagan Revolution, that missing $50,000 has largely gone into corporate profits and executive compensation—in other words, into the money bins of the nation's oligarchs.

Then there's housing. In 1980, the median home price was about $47,000, roughly three times the median (single-worker) household income. Today, the median home price exceeds $400,000, while median household (two-worker) income is around $75,000. That's more than five times the household income, and in many cities it's ten times or more. People who could have bought a home in their twenties, like Louise and I did in the 1970s, now struggle to do so even in their forties.

The same is true of education. When I attended college in the late 1960s, I paid my tuition working part-time jobs. My mom paid her way through four years at Michigan State in the 1940s working summers as a lifeguard and propping airplanes. Today's post–*Citizens United* students graduate with an average of $30,000 in debt, and total American student loan debt exceeds $1.7 trillion. We're the only developed country in the world where this is true, and an entire generation is now starting life in a financial hole that previous generations never faced.

Or consider healthcare. In 1980, healthcare costs were 8.9 percent of GDP, and most hospitals and health insurance companies were required by state law to be nonprofits. Today, healthcare costs are nearly 20 percent of GDP, and half a million American families declare bankruptcy every year just because someone got sick. Medical bankruptcy like this doesn't exist in any other developed country in the world. Only in America.

And then there are the under-siege unions. In 1980, about a third of American workers belonged to unions, so those union contracts established the wage floor for another third of American non-union workers. Today, after forty-five years of Reaganomics' relentless assault grounded in corporate constitutional rights, union membership has collapsed to around 10 percent. When workers can't organize, they can't bargain for fair wages, so corporate profits and billionaire wealth soar while workers struggle.

Perhaps most grotesque, check out wealth concentration. In 1980, the top 1 percent owned about 20 percent of all wealth. Today, they own over 35 percent. The top 0.1 percent, one in a thousand Americans, owns more wealth than the bottom 90 percent of all Americans *combined*. Just three white men own more wealth than the entire bottom half of Americans.

This is the economic and political landscape that is today's America, courtesy of corporate constitutional rights. The RAND Corporation calculated that between 1975 and 2018, fully $50 trillion was transferred from the bottom 90 percent of Americans to the top 1 percent—every penny stolen from working families and transferred to the oligarchs created by these corrupt Supreme Court decisions.[32]

| 1980 | Today |
Peak of the American Dream	After 40+ Years of Reaganomics
Middle Class: 66% of Americans	Middle Class: 43% of Americans
Adults Under 40: 21.3% of national wealth	Adults Under 40: 4.6% of national wealth
Top 1% Owned: ~20% of all wealth	Top 1% Owns: 35%+ of all wealth

The $50 Trillion Transfer:
1975–2018

Total transferred from working americans to the top 1%:
$50 trillion

That's $50,000,000,000,000
stolen from working families

CHART 9.1. Where Did the American Dream Go?
Sources: RAND Corporation, Federal Reserve, Pew Research Center

That's not capitalism or even so-called free markets. It's naked theft, enabled by made-up corporate constitutional rights and protected by a political system that the nation's wealthiest corporations now control.

These numbers should have sparked revolution. When two-thirds of wealth gains go to the top 1 percent, when working families can't afford what their parents had, when the American Dream visibly dies, studies and history show that such inequality provokes mass movements that topple oligarchies.

So how did they get away with it? How did they steal fifty trillion dollars in broad daylight without facing a democratic revolt?

They had a strategy that involved deflection, scapegoating, and blaming their victims, making sure the anger went elsewhere.

The Cover-Up and Deflection Scam

As Reagan's Revolution destroyed the union movement, transferred over $50 trillion from working-class people into the money bins of the top 1 percent, and crushed the middle class, people began to get angry.

They saw their pensions dissolved in corporate bankruptcies, their jobs sent to foreign factories, and their wages essentially frozen for more than four decades. Opportunities faded, education became absurdly expensive, healthcare started bankrupting families, and a simmering rage began to fill America.

Responding to this, the GOP and their oligarch-owned media began a multi-decade campaign to blame the collapse of the middle class first on women and Black people entering the workforce, then on immigrants, and generally on "liberals" and "socialists."

It's a strategy that's worked for fascist regimes in the past: Hitler, Mussolini, Putin, and Orbán all did the same. And it was effective enough to get Trump elected twice.

But the deflection scam and the cover-up it concealed is starting to crack under the scrutiny of a new generation of young Americans. They're figuring out what happened and how it came about, even if most don't know the nineteenth-century backstory.

The simple reality is that the American Dream didn't fade away: it was murdered, and corporate constitutional rights were the murder weapon.

10

The Cover-Up

How They Pinned the Crime on Scapegoats

RECENTLY, AN AFICIONADO OF FOX "NEWS" CALLED INTO MY RADIO program to say that he was "sick and tired of being ripped off by these Somali [Black] welfare cheats."

I asked him if he realized that from an average taxpayer's point of view, the amount of federal tax dollars that goes to everyday safety-net programs like SNAP or basic welfare "is about $324 per taxpayer, but direct subsidies and special tax breaks that favor big businesses and industries cost each taxpayer thousands of dollars per year."[33]

He grunted, as if he didn't believe me, and hung up the phone. These guys are truly well indoctrinated, which raises the question: how and why did that happen?

Reagan and the oligarchs who funded him were faced with a problem of growing discontent among "the rabble."

The billionaires and giant corporations had largely accomplished their initial goals by the end of Reagan's first term, and by Trump's second, had almost completely subdued the middle class. They'd crushed unions, slashed their own taxes to almost nothing (both personal and corporate), and shipped millions of good-paying jobs overseas to low-wage countries.

They'd turned healthcare from a nonprofit public good (by law in most states) into a $5 trillion-a-year profit center, and hedge funds, big banks, and foreign investors had transformed single-family housing into a virtual casino where the house—themselves—always won. They'd successfully transferred over fifty trillion dollars from working Americans into their own money bins in fewer than forty years.

As planned, the American Dream was dying before average people's eyes at the same time the oligarchs had become richer than any kings or emperors or pharaohs in world history. Wages stagnated while productivity—and, thus, profits—soared. Young people couldn't afford to buy their first homes. Medical debt made a fortune for the industry but bankrupted over a half million families every year. Because of all this, the middle class had shrunk from 66 percent to 43 percent in a mere four decades.

This created the problem for oligarch-owned Republican politicians: the result of all this was that people were justifiably angry—seriously pissed off. It was the kind of anger that, throughout history, has toppled oligarchies, brought down governments, and forced the rewriting of constitutions. America had become a boiling pot, and the oligarchs were starting to feel the heat.

So, they did what oligarchs have always done from the days of the Caesars to the Confederacy: they deflected that anger.

Not toward themselves, of course, even though they were the ones actually responsible for the theft of the American Dream. Not toward the corporations that were using ill-gotten constitutional rights to crush workers and capture control of most of our government. And not toward the billionaires whose assets exploded while everyone else's shrank.

Instead, they deflected the working class's anger downward, toward the very, very convenient people at the bottom of the ladder, the people with even less power than the tens of millions of struggling workers.

It was a massive cover-up of the theft of human rights, a very specific plan for blaming the victims instead of the perpetrators.

Republicans created, in other words, scapegoats.

Turning Poverty into a Moral Failure

The first move in the corporate oligarchs' cover-up playbook was to use their political platforms and captured media to make poverty shameful and government help something that everybody should become suspicious of.

Reagan didn't invent racism or disdain for the poor, of course, but he weaponized both with a fictional character: the "welfare queen." In speech after speech all across the country and in TV appearances, the Gipper described a woman in Chicago who supposedly had "eighty names, thirty addresses, twelve Social Security cards," and collected "over $150,000" every year in government benefits. She drove a "big" Cadillac, then a status symbol in the Black community. She was, Reagan told us, living large off us sucker average working-class taxpayers.

The story was almost entirely fabricated. But for Reagan's purposes, it didn't need to be true: it only needed to be useful. "Fraud" became the GOP's favorite word for everything from suppressing the vote to cutting benefits to blaming the death of the middle class on poor and Black people.

And it was devastatingly useful. That single story, told over and over again for eight years, transformed America's social safety net—so carefully constructed from the New Deal to the Great Society that had lifted millions out of poverty—from a source of security for struggling families into a "scam" that "cheaters" exploited. This victim blaming made poverty a character flaw rather than a product of the GOP's new system of low wages, union busting, expensive college, unpredictable medical costs, and soaring housing prices.

The "personal responsibility" narrative followed this vilification of poor people as naturally as leaves sprouting in the spring. If poverty was a moral failure, if struggling families were in the straits they found themselves because of "bad choices," then, Republicans and their conservative media told us, cutting programs that help them isn't cruelty, it's tough love. It's actually doing them a favor by incentivizing better behavior.

I remember how Rush Limbaugh used to tell this joke (one of his favorites when he wasn't blaming women for the economic problems of white men): "What do you do for a man when he's down? You kick him! Otherwise, he won't get up! Hahahaha!"

Notice what this narrative doesn't mention: stagnant wages, union busting, exploding healthcare and education costs, skyrocketing housing prices, offshored jobs, or any of the *actual* causes of economic insecurity brought to us by the Reagan Revolution, powered by corporate constitutional rights based on Davis's headnote. It instead keeps working-class anger focused on other working-class people—the ones getting "handouts"—while the oligarchs quietly pocket another trillion dollars.

It was the old story of the fat-cat corporate CEO sitting at a table with two working men, each with a plate before him. The CEO has a huge pile of cookies, and each of the two workers has a single cookie on his plate. The CEO points to one of them and says to the other, "Look out, he wants your cookie!"

The Southern Strategy and "Law and Order"

That well-known cookie meme also has a variation, where one worker is Black and the other is white. The CEO points at the Black worker and tells the white worker the Black guy wants to steal his cookie.

Reagan's welfare queen imagery wasn't racially neutral by a long shot. Everyone knew who Reagan was describing, just like when he'd ask people if they got angry when a "young buck" was in front of them in the supermarket line "buying steak with food stamps while all you can afford is hamburger."

The cover-up and deflection playbook has always had a racial dimension, but after the legal and political successes of the Civil Rights Movement in the 1960s and 1970s, explicit racism became politically toxic.

So Republican strategists developed what Nixon called his Southern Strategy, which Reagan cheerfully adopted in his first speech after his nomination in 1980. It was about "states' rights" near the scene of the *Mississippi Burning* murder of three civil rights workers.

It was elegant in its simplicity, a deliberate shift from explicit racism to barely coded language that activated the same resentments while maintaining a veneer of plausible deniability that could be used with great indignation in media appearances when Republicans were accused of playing the race card.

Lee Atwater, the Republican strategist who managed George H.W. Bush's 1988 campaign and created the infamous Willie Horton ad, explained it with unusual candor in a 1981 interview: "You start out in 1954 by saying, 'N*****, n*****, n*****.' By 1968 you can't say 'n*****'—that hurts you, backfires. So, you say stuff like, uh, forced busing, states' rights, and all that stuff, and you're getting so abstract. Now, you're talking about cutting taxes, and all these things you're talking about are totally economic things, and a byproduct of them is, Blacks get hurt worse than whites."[34]

"Law and order" thus became the perfect dog whistle for the men who financed the GOP and ran corporate America to pin blame on their victims. It sounds like a universal value—after all, who's against law and order?—but white working-class voters clearly understood who the "criminals" were supposed to be. Saying "predators" and "inner cities" served the same function, as did "urban" and Trump's favorite word, "thugs."

The genius of this strategy is that it lets politicians get white working-class voters to form or join coalitions that then explicitly act against their own economic interests. When voters are taught to fear "criminals" and associate them with Black or brown people, it becomes easier to justify punitive kick-them-while-they're-down policies while ignoring the economic crimes that actually drained the white communities: wage theft, predatory lending, monopoly pricing, and massive corporate and billionaire tax evasion.

Immigrants as the All-Purpose Villain

When Donald Trump launched his presidential campaign in 2015, he left behind Nixon's and Reagan's Black scapegoats and carefully chose new blame-shifting villains for his political narrative: "When Mexico sends its people, they're not sending their best.... They're bringing drugs. They're bringing crime. They're rapists."

This wasn't policy analysis; it was what is called *priming* in psychology and political science. Trump told working-class Americans who to blame for their stagnant wages, their insecure jobs, their inability to afford the life their parents had and it, for sure, wasn't the white billionaires like himself and his buddies.

The framing in this particular scapegoating strategy is always the same: *desperate people crossing borders are the problem.* Forget about the employers who hire them at below-minimum under-the-table wages. Ignore the contractors who exploit them. It's got nothing to do with the billionaire donors who benefit from weakened labor standards in GOP administrations. And the problem couldn't possibly be the oligarchs who shipped their factories overseas and then complained that American workers wanted too much money.

Border spectacles serve the blame-the-victim deflection perfectly, and Republicans provoked them by loudly proclaiming every time a Democrat was elected president that "the border is wide open." That message didn't stay in America; it drew millions to America in search of a better life. As Fox "News" found, images of "caravans" and people climbing walls or wading across rivers make great television because they trigger fear responses and personalize the "threat" of "invasion."

Meanwhile, the real immigration enforcement that would actually help raise up labor markets—going after the wealthy white oligarchs and their corporations that systematically hire undocumented workers to undercut wages—almost never happens because that would hurt the oligarchs' bottom line.

"Taxpayer" Politics:
Replace "Tax the Rich" with "They're Taking Your Stuff"

The shift to "taxpayer" language was one of the most effective blame-the-victim deflections in the oligarch's playbook.

Instead of *citizens* or *Americans* or *the public*, Republican political discourse starting in the 1980s increasingly used the word *taxpayers*. This seems neutral to most people, but in reality, it changed everything.

When you're a *taxpayer*, the government isn't serving you; it's taking "payments" from you. Public services aren't shared resources you benefit from; they're expenditures you're forced to fund. Other citizens, particularly those in distress, aren't neighbors in a shared democracy; they're potential drains on "your" money.

Most insidiously, the GOP's taxpayer language treats billionaires and middle-class workers as if they're the same person. Both are taxpayers. As a result, both are supposedly burdened equally by government spending.

It's an elegant way to get working-class people to take the political side of the billionaire class.

This is, of course, absurd. The working-class family paying 22 percent in income taxes while struggling to afford healthcare has nothing in common with the billionaire whose effective tax rate is lower than his secretary's. But taxpayer language creates this false solidarity between them and directs working-class anger at the poor, the immigrants, and anyone receiving government benefits (other than, of course, the corporations and billionaires).

There's a series of popular memes on social media that push back on these, although most will get you banned (or at least aggressively attacked) on several of the billionaire-owned platforms. Several of them make points that run along these lines:

† You're much closer to needing food stamps than you are to becoming a billionaire.

† When someone makes $60,000/year, $36 of their taxes pays for SNAP. And $700 of it pays for corporate subsidies. Poor people aren't the problem. Billionaires are.

† Who is the one taking advantage? Is it the single mom who needs to make sure her kids eat? Or is it the billion-dollar companies that collect government subsidies while they pay starvation wages to their employees who have to rely on food stamps to survive?

† I'd prefer that everyone got food stamps rather than a single billionaire gets a new mega yacht.

† Working-class people deserve joy too. Why are you judging what's in the grocery carts of EBT recipients? And aren't they allowed to have smartphones? How can you be so upset with working people when billionaires are robbing you blind?

† If you honestly object to your taxes feeding people, but you're okay with funding vacations, second homes, tanks, jets, and wars—maybe *you're* the problem.

† In a world where children go hungry, people work full time and still can't pay their rent, and basic human rights are considered luxuries, we do not need billionaires.

Billionaires like Trump successfully redirected anger that should be aimed at their oligarchic capture of government—at them and corporations paying nothing in income taxes while regular people fund the roads, schools, and courts they use—to whomever is lowest on the ladder and easiest to blame.

Rotating Scapegoats:
Target Specific Communities as Symbols of Threat

The oligarch's deflection playbook requires flexibility, so different scapegoats become useful at different times. (See Chart 10.1)

After 9/11, for example, rightwing media and the GOP identified Muslims as an existential threat to average middle-class people. Terrorism provided the fear, while surveillance and travel bans brought the policy response that validated it. An entire religious community became suspect as Fox "News" ran the Twin Towers being hit on a loop for months. Even though the attack shook us as a nation, it hardly justified a response that targeted a whole group of people whose only "crime" was being Muslim.

Refugees fleeing violence served similar purposes during the Obama and Trump administrations. Trump and racists around him loved to pin disease outbreaks on particular immigrant groups, along with "They're eating our cats and dogs!!!" So-called crime waves are attributed to immigrants, even though the data shows that natural-born Americans are far more likely to engage in criminal activity.

In recent years, Black Somali communities in places like Minnesota have become the targets of the day. "Somalis" has become a dog whistle in local and national political fights as a way to trigger fear of difference, to treat an entire community as suspect, and to mobilize voters with fear so they don't notice their pockets being picked.

The pattern is consistent all the way back to Reagan's exploitation of the AIDS epidemic: identify a vulnerable or minority community, associate it with a threat, and then use that threat to justify TV performance–style crackdowns while diverting our attention away from the actual sources of economic pain.

The Scapegoats vs. the Actual Perpetrators

Who They Blame *(The Scapegoats)*	Who Actually Did It *(The Perpetrators)*
"Illegal Immigrants" Median household wealth: ~$7,000	America's Billionaires Average individual wealth: $8.6 billion (1.2 million times larger)
"Welfare Queens" Total SNAP benefits/year: ~$113 billion	The Top 1% Combined wealth: $45 trillion (~400 times larger)
"The Poor" Bottom 50% of Americans: ~2% of wealth (~165 million people)	Just *Three* Men Bezos, Musk, Zuckerberg: More than bottom 50% (55 million times larger) (3 people vs. 165 million)

The Verdict:

† Immigrants didn't kill the American Dream.

† Welfare recipients didn't kill the American Dream.

† Poor people didn't kill the American Dream.

† Corporate constitutional rights and the oligarchs who use them killed the American Dream.

Who benefits when you blame the scapegoats?
The same people who stole the $50 trillion.

CHART 10.1. Who Killed the American Dream?
Sources: Federal Reserve, Forbes, USDA, Census Bureau

11

The Deflection Playbook

Culture War as a Substitute
for Economic Reform

PERHAPS THE MOST SOPHISTICATED DEFLECTION REPUBLICANS mobilized to conceal the corporate theft of human rights is the so-called culture war itself.

"Woke" has become the oligarch's all-purpose enemy because it's a flexible label that can be applied to civil rights advocacy, diversity initiatives, LGBTQ equality, labor activism, honest history, and even environmental protection. Anything, in other words, that the oligarchs want to discredit.

The brilliance of "anti-woke" politics is that it lets politicians rally backlash while never talking about taxes, wages, monopolies, or healthcare. Instead of debating whether hedge funds should be allowed to buy up single-family homes, we find ourselves debating whether schools should have books about diverse families. Instead of confronting pharmaceutical companies charging Americans ten times what Europeans pay for the same drugs, we argue with each other about what pronouns people should use.

Attacks on schools, libraries, and public institutions serve the same purpose for oligarchs and predatory corporations. If you can convince people that schools are "indoctrinating" their children, that libraries are "grooming" them, and that universities are "brainwashing" them, you delegitimize the very institutions that might teach people to question their oligarchic power.

The goal of these memes and the constant flood of moral-outrage stories isn't really to protect children or preserve "family values." It's to prevent any sort of economic solidarity from forming by keeping people divided over the phony issue of cultural identity.

"Fraud" Narratives That Justify Voter Suppression

The deflection playbook even extends to our democracy itself.

When elections are framed as inherently fraudulent—when "illegal votes" become the explanation for any Republican loss—it gets a whole lot easier to justify restrictive voting rules that drive down turnout. Voter ID requirements disproportionately affect poor voters, while the GOP has been on a fifty-year voter roll–purging binge going back to the days of William Rehnquist's Operation Eagle Eye that mostly targets communities of color.[35]

Reporter Greg Palast reports that Black people are 400 percent more likely to have their ballots thrown out than white people; months before the 2000 election in Florida, Governor Jeb Bush had around ninety thousand Black people purged from that state's voting rolls, giving room for his brother George to win the state by 537 votes.

Using data from the US Elections Assistance Commission, Palast discovered that voter suppression led to 14.1 million voters having their ballots disqualified in the 2024 election that Trump "won" by a margin of only two million votes.[36]

Around five million voters were purged from voter rolls without credible justification in the months leading up to the election, and another two million mail-in ballots were challenged by Republican "poll monitors" and then disqualified for minor clerical errors (e.g., postage due). Another roughly eight hundred thousand ballots were disqualified or rejected for other, non-credible reasons, and over 3.24 million new registrations were rejected in 2024 without credible evidence.[37]

"Fraud" also supposedly justifies reducing polling places in urban areas and doing away with drop boxes, while also limiting early voting and vote by mail.

The actual evidence of voter fraud in America is vanishingly small, as study after study has found that fraudulent voting is extremely rare and there's not a single election in our lifetimes that's been flipped because of it. But evidence isn't the point for the oligarchs. The goal is to make voting itself suspect, to thus create a pretext for rules that make it harder and harder for working-class people and minorities to participate in our democracy.

Corporations support these policies because if working-class people voted in proportion to their numbers—if they weren't suppressed and gerrymandered and discouraged—they'd almost certainly vote for economic policies that threaten oligarchic power. As we saw in New York City in 2005, they'd vote to tax wealth, strengthen unions, regulate corporations, and rebuild the social contract.

War, the Ultimate Deflection

In 1999, when George W. Bush decided he was going to run for president in the 2000 election, his family hired ghostwriter Mickey Herskowitz to pen the first draft of Bush's autobiography, *A Charge to Keep*.

Although Bush had gone AWOL for about a year during the Vietnam War and was thus apparently no fan of combat, he'd concluded (from watching his father's "little three-day war" with Iraq) that being a "wartime president" was the most consistently surefire way to get reelected (if you did it right) and have a two-term presidency.

Herskowitz told reporter Russ Baker in 2004:

> I'll tell you, he was thinking about invading Iraq in 1999....One of the things [Bush] said to me is: "One of the keys to being seen as a great leader is to be seen as a commander-in-chief. My father had all this political capital built up when he drove the Iraqis out of (Kuwait), and he wasted it....If I have a chance to invade Iraq, if I had that much capital, I'm not going to waste it. I'm going to get everything passed I want to get passed and I'm going to have a successful presidency.

The attack on 9/11 gave Bush his first chance to be seen as a commander-in-chief when our guy Osama bin Laden—who the Reagan/

Bush administration had spent $3 billion building up in Afghanistan—engineered an attack on New York and DC.[38]

The crime was planned in Germany and Florida.[39] On 9/11 bin Laden was, according to CBS News, not even in Afghanistan: "CBS Evening News has been told that the night before the September 11 terrorists' attack, Osama bin Laden was in Pakistan. He was getting medical treatment with the support of the very military that days later pledged its backing for the US war on terror in Afghanistan." When the Obama administration finally caught and killed bin Laden, he was again in Pakistan, the home base for the Taliban.[40]

But attacking our ally Pakistan in 2001 would have been impossible for Bush, and, besides, nearby Afghanistan was an easier target, being at that time the second-poorest country in the world with an average annual per-capita income of $700 a year. Bin Laden had run al-Qaeda training camps there, unrelated to 9/11, but they made a fine excuse for Bush's first chance to "be seen as a commander-in-chief" and get some leadership cred.

Trump reprised the strategy in 2025, becoming the first American president to bomb seven different countries in one year prior to his 2026 invasion of Venezuela and bombing of Iran. Keep them occupied with the external enemy, and they'll fail to notice who's draining their bank accounts and stealing their wages.

Breaking the Spell

Every element of this oligarch's deflection playbook serves a single purpose: preventing working-class solidarity.

The oligarchs know that they're outnumbered and that if working people across racial, religious, and cultural lines ever united around their shared economic interests, oligarch power would crumble. The deflection playbook was created and is maintained to make sure that never happens.

White workers are taught to resent Black workers. Native-born workers are taught to fear immigrant workers. Rural workers are taught to despise urban workers. Christian workers are taught to distrust Muslim workers. Straight workers are taught to feel threatened by LGBTQ workers.

All of us are taught by oligarch media to blame each other for the declining American Dream, while never, ever mentioning the actual oligarchs and their corporations who actually killed it.

Corporate constitutional rights gave the oligarchs the legal weapons they needed to destroy unions, slash taxes, offshore jobs, and capture control of our government. The deflection playbook and Reagan's ending the Fairness Doctrine gave them the necessary propaganda tools to prevent working-class people from ever launching a democratic response.

While the constitutional amendment we need to pass will strip corporations of their legal weapons, we also need to strip the oligarchs of these propaganda weapons.

That means calling out and naming these types of deflections when we see them.

12

How to Undo the Crime

Restoring the Dream

IN 1944, FRANKLIN ROOSEVELT PROPOSED A SECOND BILL OF RIGHTS. He called them economic rights, rights that would guarantee the American Dream to every citizen.

- † The right to a useful and remunerative job.
- † The right to earn enough to provide adequate food and clothing and recreation.
- † The right of every farmer to raise and sell his products at a return that would give his family a decent living.
- † The right of every businessman, large and small, to trade in an atmosphere of freedom from unfair competition and domination by monopolies.
- † The right of every family to a decent home.
- † The right to adequate medical care and the opportunity to achieve and enjoy good health.
- † The right to adequate protection from the economic fears of old age, sickness, accident, and unemployment.
- † The right to a good education.

We came close to achieving that vision, even though Republicans fought FDR tooth and nail during that era. By 1980, two-thirds of Americans lived it, until America's oligarchs and corrupt Republicans on the Supreme Court used corporate constitutional rights to take it away.

We can get it back. But first, we have to undo their crime.

The constitutional amendment to end corporate constitutional rights is one way we can undo the crime. It's how we restore democratic control over corporations. It's how we rebuild the conditions that made the American Dream possible.

Right now, we can begin waking people up. A movement is building that we can join. The crime of corporate constitutional rights can be undone. The fraud can be exposed, our democracy can be restored, and with it, the American Dream.

It will, however, ultimately require a constitutional amendment. Nothing less will work in a way that can't be challenged by corrupt, on-the-take individuals on the Supreme Court, just as Clarence Thomas became the deciding vote on *Citizens United* after taking millions in naked bribes from an interested billionaire.

And constitutional amendments, while difficult, are not impossible. America has passed twenty-seven of them. We can pass a twenty-eighth or, if the Equal Rights Amendment gets there first, a twenty-ninth.

This isn't just about democracy or corporate power in the abstract. It's also about whether our children and grandchildren will have the opportunities that previous generations enjoyed. It's about whether hard work will be rewarded with security. It's about whether the American Dream can be rebuilt.

Why a Constitutional Amendment Is Necessary

Some people ask: can't the Supreme Court just reverse *Citizens United*? Can't Congress pass a law? Can't states regulate corporations more strictly?

The answers are these: theoretically, yes; practically, maybe; and not effectively, in the largest sense.

The Supreme Court could reverse *Citizens United*, although that would require a different Court composition. But even reversing *Citizens United* wouldn't undo corporate constitutional rights: it would just limit one manifestation of it (campaign financing). Corporations would still have Fourth Amendment rights, Fifth Amendment rights, Fourteenth Amendment rights, and so on.

Congress could pass laws regulating corporate political spending, as it did back in the 1970s after the Nixon and Agnew bribery scandals. But those laws would be challenged as violating corporate First Amendment rights and with the current Court, they'd likely be struck down.

States could try to regulate corporations more strictly. But corporations would sue, claiming their constitutional rights were violated. State regulation faces the same obstacle as federal regulation: corporate constitutional rights block it.

Only a constitutional amendment can solve this in one fell swoop. An amendment would clarify that constitutional rights belong to human beings only, stripping corporations of the constitutional weapons they've been using against democracy for 140 years.

The Text of the Amendment

The organization Move to Amend has drafted a constitutional amendment that would reverse corporate constitutional rights and establish that money is not speech. Here is the proposed text:

> **Section 1.** The rights protected by the Constitution of the United States are the rights of natural persons only. Artificial entities established by the laws of any State, the United States, or any foreign state shall have no rights under this Constitution and are subject to regulation by the People, through Federal, State, or local law.
>
> The privileges of artificial entities shall be determined by the People, through Federal, State, or local law, and shall not be construed to be inherent or inalienable.
>
> **Section 2.** Federal, State, and local government shall regulate, limit, or prohibit contributions and expenditures, including a

candidate's own contributions and expenditures, to ensure that all citizens, regardless of their economic status, have access to the political process, and that no person gains, as a result of their money, substantially more access or ability to influence in any way the election of any candidate for public office or any ballot measure.

Federal, State, and local government shall require that any permissible contributions and expenditures be publicly disclosed.

The judiciary shall not construe the spending of money to influence elections to be speech under the First Amendment.

This amendment does two essential things: First, it clarifies that constitutional rights belong to natural persons (human beings) only. Corporations, LLCs, and other artificial entities would have only those privileges granted by law, which can be regulated or revoked by democratic processes. Second, it establishes that money is not speech and that government can regulate political spending to ensure equal democratic participation.

The Four Pillars to Creating Oligarchy

The Davis headnote didn't just steal constitutional rights from us humans and give them to corporations. It also handed America's oligarchs a legal toolkit that they'd use, a century later in the opening days of the Reagan Revolution (and use on steroids with Trump's second regime), to dismantle democracy itself.

For oligarchy to succeed, political scientists have identified four essential elements that the morbidly rich need to seize control of a democracy and convert it into purely oligarchic rule by and for themselves.

First, they must take control of the media so they can control and shape what people know and believe. Second, they must legalize bribery so they can buy politicians and their parties. Third, they need to pack the courts so oligarch-friendly judges will rule in their favor. And fourth, when the oligarchy is mature and ready to make the final transition to tyranny, they must seize the executive branch and use it to build a police state.

Corporate constitutional rights made three of those four possible.

Media consolidation happened because corporations successfully claimed First Amendment rights to buy Congress's and Bill Clinton's approval of the Telecommunications Act of 1996, ending ownership caps on radio and TV stations and newspapers. That's how we went from fifty media companies in 1983 to six today, and why social media platforms no longer have liability for the content that appears on them.[41]

That legalized bribery happened because the Supreme Court declared that corporate political spending was protected speech in *Buckley, Bellotti,* and *Citizens United.* Each one built on Davis's fraudulent foundation to turn money into speech, and bribery into a constitutional right.

And the courts? The oligarchs spent forty years and multiple billions of dollars building the Federalist Society and other institutions to capture the judiciary. Corporate constitutional rights gave them the legal arguments they needed.

Every time any government—federal, state, or local—tried to regulate corporate behavior, corporate lawyers jumped in to claim due process violations, takings without compensation, and/or violations of corporate free speech rights under the First Amendment.

Thus, when you look at how America became an oligarchy, we find we can't just blame greedy billionaires or corrupt politicians; we must also consider the legal foundation that made it all possible. And that's J.C. Bancroft Davis, Justice Stephen Field, and the fraudulent headnote that turned corporations into people with constitutional rights.

That's why a constitutional amendment isn't just one reform among many but is, instead, the key that unlocks everything else. Pull out corporate personhood, and the whole oligarchic structure starts to collapse.

The Path to Ratification

Constitutional amendments require the following:

1. A two-thirds vote in both the House and Senate, or a constitutional convention called by two-thirds of state legislatures.

2. Ratification by three-fourths of state legislatures (thirty-eight states).

This is a high bar, but not impossibly high. Amendments have passed on issues ranging from voting rights to prohibition to term limits. The strategy involves three parallel tracks.

Track 1: Build Public Support

Public opinion polls consistently show that 75 to 80 percent of Americans, across party lines, believe corporations shouldn't have the same rights as people and that money shouldn't dominate elections.

Out of more than twenty-four thousand attempts, Congress has successfully amended the Constitution only eighteen times in our nation's history (the first time was for all ten amendments in the Bill of Rights). In six of those instances, Congress (representing We the People) used the amendment process to directly overthrow or reverse the will of the Court, just as this would do.

The process of amending the Constitution can be drawn out, and even bloody. The Twenty-Seventh Amendment regulating congressional pay, for example, was first introduced to Congress in 1791 but not ratified until 1992. The Thirteenth, Fourteenth, and Fifteenth Amendments wouldn't exist if hundreds of thousands of Americans hadn't died fighting in the Civil War to secure those rights.

The Equal Rights Amendment, introduced in 1972, is still three states short of ratification. This single-sentence amendment simply says, "Equality of rights under the law shall not be denied or abridged by the United States or by any state on account of sex," which is strongly supported by an overwhelming majority of Americans.

When the public sentiment is strong, though, Congress and the states can move fast. For example, consider the Twenty-Sixth Amendment which lowered the voting age to eighteen. It was first introduced in Congress on March 10, 1971, and ratified just four months later on July 1: a record for the process.

FDR first proposed lowering the voting age during World War II, and Georgia lowered its voting age to eighteen in 1943. Eisenhower called for it in his State of the Union address in 1954, and Richard Nixon endorsed it too. But those of us who remember the 1970s and the Vietnam War give

TABLE 12.1. How Long Did It Take for Amendments to Pass?

Amendment	Date Proposed	Date Ratified	Months
11th	March 4, 1794	February 7, 1795	~11
12th	December 9, 1803	June 15, 1804	~6
13th	January 31, 1865	December 6, 1865	~10
15th	February 26, 1869	February 3, 1870	~11
17th	May 13, 1912	April 8, 1913	~11
20th	March 2, 1932	December 5, 1933	~11
21st	February 20, 1933	December 5, 1933	~9½
23rd	June 16, 1960	March 29, 1961	~9
26th	March 23, 1971	July 1, 1971	~3

a lot of the credit to Barry McGuire's version of "Eve of Destruction," with P.F. Sloan's haunting lyric, "You're old enough to kill, but not for voting."

Released in 1965, the song quickly hit the Billboard Top 100, and when I was working as a DJ in 1969 and 1970, it was one of the most frequently requested and played of the hourly "golden oldies." It helped galvanize a movement that crested in the spring of 1971.

While there's no big hit song today complaining about how the Supreme Court simply invented the twin doctrines of *corporate constitutional rights* and *money is free speech*, there is a broad and substantial movement across the nation to amend the Constitution to roll back both.

And fully nine of the eighteen times amendments passed, it was done in fewer than twelve months, as seen in Table 12.1.

To succeed, our movement needs to convert 140-plus years of latent support into active demand. This means education campaigns explaining corporate constitutional rights and its impacts, local organizing showing how corporate power affects communities, and media coverage of the issue and the amendment campaign.

It means, in other words, making corporate constitutional rights a defining political issue for this generation.

Track 2: Local and State Action

Hundreds of communities have already passed resolutions or ordinances declaring that corporations are not people and money is not speech. This includes cities like Los Angeles, Chicago, and Seattle, as well as dozens of small towns across America.

Twenty-two states have now called for a constitutional amendment to overturn *Citizens United*, and more are considering it.

These local and state actions don't directly change constitutional law, but they do three crucial things: they demonstrate public demand for change, educate communities about the issue, and create political pressure on the nation's politicians.

Track 3: Congressional Action

While multiple versions of constitutional amendments to address corporate constitutional rights and campaign finance have been introduced in Congress, none have yet passed.

Passage, of course, requires first building political will. That means electing representatives who support the amendment, pressuring existing representatives to support it, making opposition to the amendment politically costly, and creating a political environment where representatives can't afford to oppose it.

The Opposition

This generation's American oligarchs and their corporations have already proven they'll fight this amendment with everything they have. They will

> **Claim it violates free speech.** They'll argue that limiting corporate political spending violates the First Amendment. This is circular reasoning. The amendment exists precisely because corporate "free speech" claims are illegitimate.

Claim it will hurt the economy. They'll say that regulating corporations will destroy business, kill jobs, and ruin prosperity. This is nonsense. The amendment doesn't prevent corporations from doing business; it simply prevents them from claiming constitutional rights to override democratic governance.

Claim it's unnecessary. They'll say there are better ways to address corporate power. But 140-plus years of trying other approaches have failed. Only a constitutional amendment can fix what Davis's fraudulent headnote broke.

Spend unlimited money opposing it. This is the real danger. Because *Citizens United* also gave foreign oligarchs and corporations the "right" to finance and influence US political campaigns, American and foreign oligarchs will fund massive propaganda campaigns, buy politicians, and use every corporate constitutional right they have to prevent the amendment from passing.

The irony is rich: corporations claiming First Amendment rights will use those very stolen rights to prevent an amendment that would eliminate those rights.

The Grassroots Strategy

The amendment will pass only through grassroots organizing. Oligarchs control the top-down power structures: media, money, and politicians. But they can't control millions of people organizing at the local level.

The strategy that worked for other major movements—including abolition, women's suffrage, unionization, and civil rights—will work here:

Educate. Tell everybody you know the story of Davis's fraudulent headnote and the theft of human constitutional rights, along with their impact.

Start Local. Get your city council or town meeting to pass a resolution supporting the amendment. This educates your community and creates momentum.

Go to Your State Legislature. Push your state representatives to pass a resolution calling for the amendment. Twenty-two states have done this, but thirty-eight are needed.

Pressure Your Congressional Representatives. Make them take a position. If they oppose the amendment, make that opposition costly at the ballot box.

Organize Your Community. Start a local Move to Amend chapter and join Public Citizen, which has also prioritized this movement. Host educational events. Talk to your neighbors. Build a local movement.

Connect to Other Movements. Environmental groups, labor unions, racial justice organizations, consumer advocates, small business groups: all are harmed by corporate constitutional rights. Build coalitions.

Use Corporate Overreach Against Them. Every time a corporation does something outrageous, claims religious freedom to deny employee rights, sues to block environmental regulations, or spends millions buying elections, use it as an organizing opportunity. Make the abstract concrete.

Be Persistent. Constitutional amendments take time. The women's suffrage movement started with Abigail Adams in the 1780s. The modern-era Civil Rights Movement took decades. This movement has been building for more than forty years. It will take more time.

But it will win.

The Tipping Point

Social movements don't succeed gradually. They build pressure slowly, then reach a tipping point when change happens quickly.

Slavery seemed permanent until suddenly it wasn't. Women's suffrage seemed impossible until suddenly it passed. Gay marriage seemed unthinkable until suddenly it was constitutional.

The corporate constitutional rights amendment will follow the same pattern. Years of organizing will seem to produce little visible progress.

Then suddenly, the dam will break. Public opinion will demand action. Politicians will scramble to get on the right side of history. The amendment will pass quickly once the tipping point is reached.

The question is *when*, not *if*.

And the answer to *when* depends on how many people like you join the movement now.

Alternatives to a Constitutional Amendment: Legislation

Given what a huge lift a constitutional amendment can be, there are a couple of alternatives that, at the very least, could be midpoints toward that goal.

The first is for Congress to assert its authority over the Supreme Court laid out in Article III, Section 2 of the Constitution, which reads: "In all Cases affecting Ambassadors, other public Ministers and Consuls, and those in which a State shall be Party, the supreme Court shall have original Jurisdiction. In all the other Cases before mentioned, the supreme Court shall have appellate Jurisdiction, both as to Law and Fact, *with such Exceptions, and under such Regulations as the Congress shall make*" (emphasis added).

In other words, Congress can make exceptions to what the Supreme Court may rule on, create regulations determining the size and salaries of the Court, and, to an extent, direct how they may behave.

There are some substantial limits on how far Congress could go with this, both legal/constitutional and practical. For decades, conservatives have proposed literally hundreds of bills that would strip the Supreme Court of its power. Examples of these attempts include (1) enforcing desegregation via its *Brown v. Board* decision, (2) legalizing school prayer—despite Supreme Court decisions that it violates the First Amendment ban on government-endorsed religious practices—and (3) outlawing abortion in the post-Roe era.

Every one of those attempts failed, not because they were struck down legally but, instead, because Congress could never pull together enough of a consensus to pass them. But that doesn't mean it's impossible.

After the Civil War, for example, a Mississippi newspaper editor challenged Reconstruction laws via a habeas corpus pleading, and the Supreme Court agreed to hear the case.

Congress panicked and, before the Court even ruled, repealed the statute giving the Court jurisdiction, explicitly stripping the Court of authority to decide that class of cases. As a result, the Court, in the *ex parte McArdle* case, essentially rolled over, saying that they had no choice but to do so because Congress had removed their jurisdiction.

Congress has also removed Supreme Court review in certain immigration cases, limited habeas corpus appeals (especially after the 1996 AEDPA), restricted federal court review of military tribunals, and required some constitutional disputes to go through special three-judge panels with limited appeal.

But having Congress simply repeal corporate constitutional rights by statute would be a much bigger lift because corporate constitutional rights aren't based on a single statute. Instead, they rest on constitutional interpretation (especially the Fourteenth Amendment), over a century of Supreme Court precedent, and the Court's very real authority to interpret constitutional terms such as *person* and *speech*.

Congress would, instead, have to take a more limited approach by stripping jurisdiction over future cases, narrowly defining corporate rights by law, regulating corporations more aggressively, and requiring constitutional amendments for certain privileges.

Congress can't declare the Supreme Court's constitutional interpretation void, order the Court to reinterpret the Constitution, or retroactively negate constitutional holdings by passing laws alone because all would violate the constitutionally mandated separation of powers.

Additionally, jurisdiction stripping wouldn't solve corporate constitutional rights because, even if Congress stripped the Supreme Court of jurisdiction over "corporate constitutional rights cases," lower federal courts could still apply existing precedent, state courts could still hear constitutional challenges, the old Supreme Court decisions that established precedent when they cited the *Santa Clara* headnote would remain binding, and, of course, corporations would continue asserting constitutional rights unless the Constitution itself changed.

Jurisdiction stripping could thus, on a limited basis, prevent new rulings, but it can't erase old ones.

Another legislative strategy would be to aggressively narrow corporate rights by statute. Such laws could include a ban on corporate political spending, reclassifying corporate entities for regulatory purposes, denying statutory rights that aren't constitutionally required, and forcing corporate "rights" cases into unfavorable procedural paths.

These won't repeal corporate constitutional rights but could neutralize some of their effects.

Alternatives to a Constitutional Amendment: Change the Court

The Supreme Court has famously reversed itself repeatedly throughout history. Even the post–*Santa Clara* rulings asserting corporate constitutional rights were arguably reversals of prior rulings.

Some of those reversals, or changes in the direction the Court was moving, were in response to public pressure, as I chronicle in *The Hidden History of the Supreme Court and the Betrayal of America*. The most famous was "the switch in time that saved nine" when, in 1937, a pivotal member of the Supreme Court stopped fighting and started supporting FDR's New Deal legislation. The president had publicly declared his intention to expand the Court, and public opinion was largely on his side. That was all it took to intimidate the justices into doing the right thing.

That's unlikely today, given how interwoven the Republicans on the Court have become with the interests and personalities of the billionaire GOP donors that helped each of them get their jobs.

But FDR's idea still has merit. Congress, in its capacity as a regulator of the Court, could increase the number of justices, institute term limits, and create a code of ethics that might even break that strong bond between rightwing billionaires and the Court's Republicans.

All three of those measures would, over a period of a few years, change both the composition and the behavior of the justices, and could conceivably cause them to essentially reverse, at least, the *Bellotti* and *Citizens United* decisions and their peers.

All of these non-amendment solutions, though, suffer from failing to completely reverse or end corporate constitutional rights, and they themselves could be subject to future reversals as the result of ongoing billionaire- and corporate-lobbying efforts. The most efficient method, I maintain, is to amend the Constitution.

13

What Happens After the Amendment Passes

Passing the amendment is just the beginning. Implementation will require the following:

New Legislation—Congress and state legislatures will need to pass laws (like that old Wisconsin law mentioned earlier) exercising their new regulatory authority over corporations and political spending.

Legal Challenges—Corporations will challenge these laws, trying to find loopholes. Courts will need to interpret the amendment.

Corporate Resistance—Corporations won't give up power easily. They'll seek work-arounds, create new legal structures, and test the boundaries of the amendment.

Ongoing Vigilance—The oligarchs will always try to buy back their power. Democracy requires constant defense.

But all of this is manageable. The hard part is passing the amendment. Once it's ratified, the legal framework exists to restore democratic control over corporate power.

What Becomes Possible

Ending corporate constitutional rights isn't just about restoring democracy; it's also about restoring the American Dream. When corporations lose their constitutional weapons, we can finally do what two Progressive Eras proved was possible during previous generations: build a society where hard work is rewarded, where ordinary people can own homes and start businesses, where children have opportunities their parents never had, and where the predators among us are held in check.

Here's what becomes possible:

Rebuild unions without corporate First Amendment interference. Right now, corporations claim First Amendment rights to run anti-union campaigns, to force workers to attend "captive audience" meetings, and to flood workplaces with propaganda. When corporations lose those rights, workers can organize freely. Union membership could return to the levels of 1980, before Reagan and the GOP went on the attack, and union contracts could once again set the wage floor for entire industries. That alone would reverse decades of wage stagnation.

Tax oligarchs properly without claims of unconstitutional takings. Corporations have used constitutional rights to fight taxes at every level, from local property taxes to federal income taxes. When those rights disappear and politicians again fear the voters more than their donors, we can finally tax wealth and corporate profits at rates that will fully fund public goods and pay down our national debt. We can rebuild infrastructure, fund education, and create the conditions for broad prosperity.

Make healthcare affordable by regulating monopolies. Healthcare corporations have used constitutional rights to fight regulation, to block single-payer systems, and to maintain monopoly pricing. Without those rights, we can do what every other developed nation on Earth has done—guarantee healthcare as a right, not a privilege. Medical bankruptcy could become as rare in America as it is everywhere else.

Make education accessible by properly funding it. Corporate constitutional rights have been used to fight taxes that fund public education and to challenge regulations on for-profit colleges and scam operations like Trump University that intentionally saddle students with debt. Without those rights, we can return to the days when college was affordable or free, when students could work their way through school, and when education opened doors instead of creating debt traps.

Make housing affordable by regulating investor speculation. Wall Street firms have used corporate rights to fight regulations on their purchase of single-family homes, their manipulation of rental markets, and their conversions of housing from shelter into speculative assets. Without those rights, we can regulate or prohibit corporate (including foreign corporate) ownership of residential housing, returning homes to families instead of hedge funds.

Restore competitive markets through antitrust enforcement. Corporations have used constitutional rights to fight antitrust enforcement, to challenge breakup orders, and to maintain monopoly power. Without those rights, we can enforce antitrust laws vigorously, break up the massive monopolies that now control our lives, and restore the competitive markets that will once again create opportunities for small businesses and entrepreneurs.

Rebuild local communities with living wages. Corporations have used constitutional rights to fight minimum wage increases, to challenge local living wage ordinances, and to block worker protections. Without those rights, communities can set wages that allow workers to live with dignity, to support families, and to participate in local economies.

Address climate change without corporate obstruction. Fossil fuel corporations have used constitutional rights to fight environmental regulations, to challenge carbon taxes, to buy politicians, and to block the transition to clean energy. Without those rights, we can finally take the action that science demands, preserving a livable planet for our children and grandchildren.

In short, ending corporate constitutional rights makes it possible to rebuild everything that made the American Dream real. We'll still have to organize, vote, and fight to bring all this about. But the constitutional weapons that corporations have used to block progress for 140 years will be gone, thus increasing the likelihood of our success.

The Historical Parallel

In 1865, the Thirteenth Amendment abolished slavery. In 1868, the Fourteenth Amendment granted citizenship and equal protection to freed slaves.

Both amendments overturned Supreme Court precedent (the *Dred Scott* decision). Both were passed after massive grassroots movements. Both faced enormous opposition from entrenched power. And both succeeded because ordinary people organized and persisted.

The corporate constitutional rights amendment would correct the perversion of the Fourteenth Amendment and would restore it to its original purpose: protecting human rights, not corporate power.

It would complete the unfinished work of Reconstruction.

It would undo the greatest legal crime in American history.

14

The Rebellion Has Already Begun

WE DON'T HAVE TO HOPE FOR OR IMAGINE WHAT RESISTANCE TO corporate constitutional rights might look like; it's already happening. All across America communities are fighting back against corporation constitutional rights, passing ordinances to regulate corporations, building movements based on outing Davis's fraudulent headnote and its spawn, and creating the foundation for the constitutional amendment that could restore democracy and rebuild the middle class's American Dream.

These rebellions across the country aren't simply abstract legal battles, either. They're explicit fights for the things that made America so successful for working people prior to the Reagan Revolution: good jobs that pay living wages, clean water and air, affordable housing and education, local businesses that keep wealth within their communities, and FDR's simple promise that if you work hard, you can build a decent life for yourself and your family.

These movements are led by the rebels and resisters. They're the heroes of the effort to overturn oligarchy and restore We-the-People democracy to America.

What They're Really Fighting For

When the residents of a Pennsylvania township fight against a toxic waste injection well, they're not just fighting pollution: they're battling for the health of their children, the value of their homes, and the democratic and economic future of their community. They're fighting for the American Dream that their parents and grandparents lived before Reagan: the promise that they could raise a family in a safe place, drink clean water from the tap, and pass a better America filled with opportunity for their kids.

When folks in a small town battle Walmart or Amazon, they're not just opposing a single store or warehouse. They're fighting for the locally owned businesses that sponsored Little League teams and hired neighborhood kids for summer jobs. They're trying to bring back the downtown that was the heart of their community. They're struggling against a corporate behemoth for an economy where prosperity is shared rather than extracted, and every penny rung up each day is sent to Bentonville, Arkansas, or Bezos's money bin with the touch of a button at day's end.

When communities stand up to organize against private equity firms buying up their housing, they're fighting for the simple ability to own a home, the foundation of middle-class wealth that my generation took for granted but that's slipped away from Millennials and Zoomers.

Corporate constitutional rights gave both American and foreign oligarchs the legal weapons they needed to take all of this away from average citizens. These local rebellions are, in fact, communities saying "enough" and *demanding* their American Dream back.

The Early Pioneers

The movement to challenge corporate constitutional rights at the local level began in small communities willing to take bold stands.

In 2000, Point Arena, California, became the first municipality in America to pass a ballot initiative banning corporate constitutional rights within city limits. The measure declared: "Corporations and other business entities shall not be considered to be 'persons' protected by the United States Constitution in Point Arena." The legal effect was limited, since federal constitutional law preempts local ordinances, but the political effect was enormous. A community had democratically decided that corporations should not have constitutional rights.

In 2006, Spokane, Washington, became one of the first major cities to pass an ordinance declaring that corporations are not persons entitled to constitutional rights and that the community had authority to regulate corporate activity for the public good. Corporations howled and their lawyers threatened lawsuits, but citizen activists persisted, packing council meetings and organizing until the city acted.

These early victories were largely symbolic: Spokane and Point Arena couldn't actually strip corporations of constitutional rights on their own; only a constitutional amendment or reversal by the Court itself could do that. But the symbolism mattered. Two communities had declared that corporate constitutional rights were illegitimate. Others noticed.

The Pennsylvania Revolution

The real modern revolution against corporate constitutional rights began in rural Pennsylvania.

In the late 1990s and early 2000s, townships across Pennsylvania faced an invasion. Large corporations wanted to dump toxic waste, operate industrial hog farms that poisoned wells and streams, and extract natural gas through fracking that contaminated groundwater. State and federal environmental regulations not only weren't stopping them, they often made things worse by preempting local control. Once a corporation obtained a state or federal permit, the local Pennsylvania communities had no power to say no.

This was Davis's and Field's doctrine of corporate constitutional rights, as intended, in action. Corporations claimed that their constitutional rights trumped community decisions, their property rights overrode local environmental protections, and their due process rights should make it nearly impossible for communities to protect themselves.

The Community Environmental Legal Defense Fund (CELDF) helped townships fight back with a radical strategy: pass local ordinances asserting democratic control over corporate activity within the township, regardless of state or federal permits. The ordinances declared that corporations are not persons with constitutional rights, that corporate constitutional rights cannot override community decisions, and that the community's right to clean water, clean air, and democratic self-governance trumped corporate property rights.

Thompson Township, Pennsylvania, faced a particularly aggressive threat: a massive injection well for toxic waste that would have poisoned their groundwater for generations. In 2005, the township passed an ordinance banning corporate "personhood rights" and declaring that the community had the authority to prohibit activities that threatened health, safety, and welfare. The corporation sued, claiming its constitutional rights were violated, and the court ruled in favor of the corporation. After all, under current constitutional law, corporations have rights that communities can't override.

But Thompson Township didn't back down. They revised the ordinance, kept organizing, and kept fighting. Other townships noticed: if Thompson could fight, so could they.

As a result, dozens of Pennsylvania townships passed similar ordinances. Courts struck down many of them, but the communities kept passing them because, the organizers understood, the fight itself was the point: educating, organizing, and building a movement.

The Wave Spreads

By 2010, over 150 communities across America had passed ordinances or resolutions challenging corporate constitutional rights and asserting community rights. Pittsburgh, Pennsylvania, banned natural gas drilling within city limits and declared that corporations couldn't use constitutional rights to challenge the ban. Lafayette, Colorado, banned fracking and declared corporate constitutional rights illegitimate. Mendocino County, California, banned GMO crops and stripped corporations of the constitutional right to challenge their ban.

In 2012, Barnstead, New Hampshire, passed what was perhaps the most eloquent ordinance. It began "We the People of the Town of Barnstead, New Hampshire, have the right to produce, process, sell, purchase and consume local foods thus promoting our inherent right to self-government in our community." It declared that corporations were not persons entitled to constitutional rights and that if federal or state law conflicted with the ordinance, the ordinance would control.

This was radical stuff, the kind that preceded the Boston Tea Party, with a small New Hampshire town declaring that its democratic decisions trumped corporate constitutional rights and even state and federal law. Barnstead knew the ordinance couldn't be enforced in court, but enforcement wasn't the goal. As asserted earlier, educating, organizing, and building a movement were the goals.

As a result of these early efforts, today over 725 municipalities have passed resolutions in support of ending corporate constitutional rights.[42]

More than eight hundred organizations have endorsed the We the People Amendment.[43] The pattern is consistent: communities facing corporate threats are increasingly fighting back by asserting democratic authority and denying corporations their claimed constitutional rights.

Fighting for Rural America

Across rural America, communities have been battling the massive industrial factory farms that have often destroyed the family-farm agricultural way of life that sustained generations of American families.

These new invaders aren't the farms that built the American heartland; they're giant corporate operations housing tens of thousands of hogs or chickens in concentrated facilities, generating massive amounts of waste that contaminates wells, pollutes streams, and makes the air unbreathable.

In North Carolina, corporate hog farms spray millions of gallons of liquefied pig waste onto fields, and the mist drifts into neighboring homes and schools. Families can't sit on their porches, children develop respiratory problems, and property values collapse. The American Dream of rural life often, in the face of these factory farms, becomes a nightmare.

When communities tried to fight back, corporations claimed constitutional rights to resist local control. They claimed their buying local politicians to facilitate their operations were First Amendment–protected free speech. They claimed local regulations constituted Fifth Amendment unconstitutional takings of their property. They used the weapons that

Davis's 1886 fraud gave them to override the democratic will of communities trying to protect their homes and families.

But communities are continuing to organize. They're passing local ordinances asserting their right to clean air and water. They're demanding that family farmers, not corporate operations, define their agricultural future. In this, they're fighting for the rural version of the American Dream that the agribusiness oligarchs are gleefully destroying for profit.

Fighting Big Box

When I started my first two businesses in the late 1960s and early 1970s, pretty much every store in town was locally owned. The hardware store, the pharmacy, the grocery, the clothing shops, even the banks were almost all run by local families who lived in the community, hired local kids, sponsored youth sports teams, and kept their profits circulating in the local economy.

That was the American Dream of entrepreneurship that I lived, starting five successful businesses over the years. As a result of the Reagan Revolution grounded in corporate constitutional rights, however, it's increasingly impossible today.

When a Walmart superstore opens, studies show that between 35 and 60 percent of nearby typically locally owned stores close. The Walmart jobs that replace them usually pay less and offer fewer benefits. And the revenues and profits that used to circulate in the local community keeping it healthy now flow to the Walton family in Bentonville and New York's Wall Street shareholders.

Over the past three decades, multiple communities have tried to fight back by passing ordinances limiting store sizes, requiring living wages, and even demanding environmental and traffic impact studies. But Walmart's lawyers inevitably invoke corporate constitutional rights to challenge every restriction.

In communities across America, from Vermont to California, citizens have organized to keep big-box stores out. A few have won, particularly when the local level of outrage is impossible for the giant corporations to ignore. Many others have lost. But all of them understand that what's at stake is the American Dream of locally owned businesses, local jobs that help the community, and the kind of local prosperity that supports a healthy middle class.

Fighting Private Equity

When my dad bought his first house (the one I grew up in) in the 1950s, the median home price was about 2.2 times the median annual individual income. Today it's over ten times. Single family homes, the foundation of middle-class wealth and security, have been transformed by massive out-of-town corporations from a basic need into a speculative commodity.

Private equity firms and hedge funds are buying up single-family homes across America. In some neighborhoods they've purchased half the available houses, turning homeowners into permanent renters. They use sophisticated algorithms to identify properties, make all-cash offers that families can't compete against, and then raise rents as high as the software says the market will bear.

When communities try to regulate these corporate landlords through rent control, tenant protections, or limits on corporate home purchases, the corporations invariably claim constitutional rights, property rights, due process rights, equal protection rights, and free speech rights to buy local politicians. The exact same fraudulent constitutional weapons that the railroad oligarchs, Justice Stephen Field, and court reporter J.C. Bancroft Davis manufactured in 1886 are today regularly used to price young Americans out of homeownership entirely.

Some communities are fighting back, trying to define limits on corporate ownership of residential property. Others are demanding real transparency about who really owns the local rental housing. Still others are using legal devices like community land trusts to keep housing affordable and under local control.

Ultimately, these battles are about more than just housing policy. They're fighting for an American Dream of homeownership that will survive in the face of corporate efforts to turn America into a nation of permanent renters paying monthly tribute to Wall Street landlords.

The Boardroom Rebellion

The fight against corporate political power isn't just happening in town halls and state legislatures; it's also happening in corporate boardrooms and shareholder meetings.

Since *Citizens United*, investors have been pushing corporations to disclose and account for the political spending those five corrupt Republicans on the Court legalized. For example, the Center for Political Accountability, working with the Zicklin Center for Business Ethics at the University of Pennsylvania's Wharton School, publishes an annual index ranking S&P 500 companies on their political transparency and accountability.[44]

The progress of this effort has been frankly remarkable. In 2016, only 94 S&P 500 companies scored in the top tier for political disclosure. By 2024, that number had more than doubled to 206 companies. The average disclosure score climbed from 42 percent in 2016 to nearly 60 percent in 2024. Board oversight of political spending increased from 229 companies in 2016 to 319 companies in 2024, representing more than 60 percent of the S&P 500.

In the 2025 proxy season, shareholder proposals demanding transparency of corporate political spending saw surprising successes. Proposals to disclose political campaign spending passed at five major companies, with support averaging 42 percent across all companies facing such resolutions, up dramatically from 26 percent the year before.

Americans are increasingly sick of watching their politicians purchased by massive corporations, and as a result, political spending and lobbying disclosure are now the most frequently filed proposal topics.

Again, though, this isn't the necessary constitutional amendment. These efforts don't strip corporations of constitutional rights or overturn *Citizens United*. But they nonetheless represent something critically important: even within the corporate system, pressure is building for transparency and accountability to protect our democracy. Shareholders are increasingly demanding to know the details of how corporations spend money to influence politics, and corporate boards are being held responsible for corrupting politics and governance.

The oligarchs, of course, are furious about this turn of events. Anti-ESG (Environmental, Social, and Governance) forces are pushing back hard, trying to eliminate shareholder proposals that demand political accountability. The Trump administration's Security and Exchange Commission (SEC) has even signaled hostility to the most basic of governance reforms. But the momentum built over the past few decades has proven resilient and, so far, most companies aren't backsliding.

This boardroom rebellion complements the grassroots movement to end corporate constitutional rights. It shows local citizen and shareholder fury about corporate political power crosses traditional political boundaries. Conservative investors worried about fiduciary duty find themselves aligned with progressive activists demanding democratic accountability. Both understand that unlimited, undisclosed corporate political spending both corrupts democracy and distorts markets in ways that screw consumers and communities.

The Native American Connection

Native American tribes—the original residents of this continent and the originators of many of our democratic traditions—have been fighting corporate constitutional rights and corporate power for generations.

The Navajo Nation successfully banned uranium mining on their ancient tribal lands. Numerous other tribes have rejected pipeline permits, as we saw when the Standing Rock Sioux fought the Dakota Access Pipeline.

Tribes understand something that other Americans are just now learning: sovereignty requires having democratic control over what happens in your territory, but corporate constitutional rights undermine that basic right.

Many tribes have passed resolutions supporting a constitutional amendment to abolish corporate constitutional rights, seeing the connection between their sovereignty struggles and the larger national fight for democratic control.

15

The Amendment Movement and the State Resolutions

Twenty-two states have passed resolutions calling for a constitutional amendment to address corporate constitutional rights and again regulate money in politics: Alaska, California, Colorado, Connecticut, Delaware, Hawaii, Illinois, Maine, Maryland, Massachusetts, Montana, Nevada, New Hampshire, New Jersey, New Mexico, New York, Oregon, Rhode Island, Vermont, Virginia, Washington, and West Virginia.[45]

While these resolutions vary in their specific language, all express the fundamental principle that corporations are not people, money is not speech, and a functioning democracy that meets the needs of its people *requires* limiting corporate political power.

Eighteen more states are needed to trigger a constitutional convention under Article V of the Constitution, although it must be one limited to ending corporate constitutional rights, not the movement conservatives have been pushing for four decades—one that would open the entire Constitution and rewrite it the way Ronald Reagan would want it. The movement for a convention limited to ending corporate constitutional rights is now more than halfway there.

Big Cities Join the Fight

In 2012, Los Angeles became the largest city to support a constitutional amendment overturning *Citizens United* when the City Council voted

10–1 to support the effort. Council Member Richard Alarcon cut right to the chase, saying, "Our government is being bought and sold by corporations. We need to take our democracy back."

Other major cities quickly followed: Chicago, Seattle, San Francisco, Boston, Philadelphia have all passed similar resolutions. It's a great start.

The Youth Movement

Young people, who're the most damaged by corporate constitutional rights and the corruption it produces, totally get it. They've grown up in an age of corporate domination and climate crisis and—Trump administration efforts to rewrite civics textbooks notwithstanding—increasingly understand that it's illegitimate corporate power that threatens their futures.

They also understand what was stolen from them by Davis's corrupt headnote, even if they've never heard of Davis or the *Santa Clara* case. Millennials know that Boomers at their age owned five times as much of the nation's wealth while they and Zoomers see a future of stagnant wages, crushing debt, unaffordable housing, and a climate spiraling toward catastrophe.

As a result, student groups across America are passing their own resolutions supporting a constitutional amendment to eliminate corporate constitutional rights. To the chagrin of the nation's largest corporations and the politicians they own, college campuses have become major organizing hubs.

The Strategic Debate

Within the overall anti-corporate constitutional rights movement, there's an ongoing debate about the most effective strategy and how to implement it (or them). It's a healthy debate similar to what's almost always seen early in major movements, and digging into it helps clarify what's really at stake.

On one side are the people who call themselves the abolitionists. They argue that corporate constitutional rights themselves are illegitimate on their face, and that a functioning democracy requires abolishing them altogether. Only natural persons, they'll tell you, should have constitutional rights. Move to Amend and its allies take this position, as did many of the activists whose community rights ordinances passed in Pennsylvania and elsewhere.

On the other side are the mitigators. They accept that some forms of legal corporate constitutional rights are almost certainly here to stay and that basic corporate constitutional rights have become foundational to modern commerce, but they want sharp limits on the rights corporations can claim, especially around corporate interference in elections. They're essentially arguing that we need strong regulatory and governance regimes to keep corporate power in check, and that may well be enough. The Democracy for All Amendment, which focuses specifically on campaign finance, represents this approach.

And then there are some folks who argue that focusing on ending corporate constitutional rights may itself be a strategic dead end, that the real problem is big money in politics instead of corporate constitutional rights per se, and that we can fix the former without nuking the latter.

On that, I disagree. The history I've laid out in this book demonstrates that corporate constitutional rights are pretty much exclusively at the root of the problem. *Citizens United*, for example, wasn't a cause but a symptom of this Court-created ideology. I'd point out that corporations have been claiming constitutional rights since 1886, and every time we pass laws to restrain them, they use those rights to strike the laws down. The only permanent solution, in my opinion, is to eliminate the rights themselves.

But this debate shouldn't be allowed to divide us. The abolitionists and the mitigators are on the same side: both want to end corporate domination of our politics, both want to restore democratic control, and both are ultimately fighting for a restoration of the American Dream that corporate constitutional rights have stolen from us.

Thus, the comprehensive amendment is the best and ultimate goal. But, if a narrower campaign finance amendment passes first, that's still worthy and important progress. When shareholder activism forces more corporate transparency, that's also progress. If we can convince courts to begin to narrow corporate claims to human rights, that's even more progress. Every step we take that weakens corporate political power makes the next step easier.

The Pattern: Local Action, National Impact

Every one of these local actions, ordinances, resolutions, and ballot initiatives—and there have been hundreds over the past quarter century—have had limited direct legal effect. But collectively, they're building what will hopefully become an irresistible political movement.

They demonstrate that people across America, across the political spectrum, in red states and blue states, in cities and rural areas, almost universally—when they understand how it works—want to end corporate constitutional rights and restore democracy.

These efforts have also educated and created a network of organizers who've learned how to fight corporate power at the local level. They've informed literally millions of Americans about an issue most had never heard of before the twenty-first century.

Increasingly, they're showing politicians that any continuing support for corporate constitutional rights can be politically costly.

And most importantly, they've built the foundation for that essential constitutional amendment. History tells us that we can't pass an amendment without a grassroots movement behind it, and these local actions are creating that very movement.

The Next Phase

As I hope I've laid out clearly, the rebellion against corporate power and the illegitimate constitutional rights that underlay it is growing. The question that confronts Americans now is whether it'll grow fast enough to save democracy before that corporate power becomes insurmountable and America slips into all-out fascism as defined by Mussolini: the merger of corporations and a strongman-run state.

In other words, we're now in a race against time. Corporate consolidation has been accelerating, particularly under the Trump administration.

Wealth inequality is exploding at the same time the climate crisis is intensifying. Oligarchic control of our media, our business community, and even our democratic process is tightening.

As a result, the window for successful action is narrowing.

But the rebellion is real and the movement is growing. Ordinary people are organizing all across America, rural and urban, wealthy and low income, and are fighting back. It bears repeating that the We the People Amendment has over 60 cosponsors in Congress, over 800 organizations have endorsed it, and over 725 municipalities have so far (as of this writing) passed supporting resolutions.

The oligarchs' corporate constitutional rights Field and Davis created are indeed powerful, but they're not invincible. History tells us that when enough people organize persistently enough for long enough, they win.

The rebellion has begun.

16

The Global Stakes

WHILE THIS BIZARRE DOCTRINE OF CORPORATE CONSTITUTIONAL rights began here, it's no longer just an American problem. Through trade agreements, international treaties, and the global spread of American legal concepts pushed by corporate-friendly law firms (who often "volunteer" to help other countries rewrite their laws and constitutions), American oligarchs have exported corporate constitutional rights worldwide. As a result, democracy is under assault pretty much everywhere.

But it's more than just democracy that's at stake, as vital as that is. The American Dream itself, the model of a prosperous middle class that inspired nations around the world and underpins democracy, is being systematically prevented from taking root in many other nations.

To protect their wealth and power in an increasingly interconnected world, the very same oligarchs who destroyed the American Dream here at home are now working hard to make sure no other country in the world can have a middle class economically and politically strong enough to challenge them.

Rightwing populist movements are rising in response, many funded by American and Russian oligarchs. But these movements don't blame corporate personhood or neoliberalism for the death of the middle class. Instead, they deploy the same scapegoating and deflection playbook that American oligarchs have perfected: blame immigrants, blame minorities, blame cultural change, blame anyone except the inequality and stolen human rights that actually caused the problem.

This isn't coincidental. American political strategists and oligarch-funded think tanks have exported the deflection playbook right alongside their neoliberal economics. The same techniques that Reagan used to blame "welfare queens" for America's problems are now being used to blame refugees for Europe's problems, Muslims for India's problems, and indigenous people for Brazil's problems.

The global oligarchy has learned their lesson: they can rob countries blind so long as they give their people someone powerless to blame.

The Export of Corporate Rights

For most of the twentieth century, corporate constitutional rights were primarily an American idiosyncrasy. Right up until the 1980s, other democracies never granted their corporations the equivalent of our constitutional rights. Britain, France, Germany, Japan all treated corporations as legal entities subject to democratic regulation, not as rights-bearing "persons."

Then came Reagan's and Clinton's joint embrace of neoliberal globalization, and with it, the aggressive export of American corporate law that's repeatedly based in corporate constitutional rights.

Through the World Bank, International Monetary Fund, and World Trade Organization, American politicians and corporate lawyers forced a model of corporate-friendly law onto developing nations. Want a loan? You must adopt legal structures that protected corporate property rights. Want trade agreements? You must accept that corporations could override local regulations.

The same oligarchs who corrupted American democracy with Davis's corrupt headnote thus began corrupting democracy worldwide.

The Global Race to the Bottom

More often than not, modern trade agreements prevent other countries from building the kind of middle class that America built between 1933 and 1981.

Consider how we first created the American Dream with FDR's New Deal and LBJ's Great Society. Strong unions could bargain for living wages. Regulations protected workers from exploitation. Taxes on the morbidly rich funded public education, infrastructure, and social safety nets. Trade policies and rational tariffs passed after deliberation by Congress protected domestic manufacturing. All of it together constrained corporate power and distributed prosperity more broadly across America.

The post-Reagan trade agreements, however, almost universally give corporations the right to sue governments that try to raise wages, strengthen environmental protections, or have the temerity to try to regulate corporate behavior. As a result, over the past thirty-or-so years oligarchs worldwide have created a race to the bottom where less wealthy countries compete to offer the lowest wages, the weakest regulations, and the most favorable treatment to multinational corporations.

If Mexico tries to strengthen its labor laws, corporations threaten to move to Vietnam. If Vietnam raises environmental standards, corporations threaten to move to Bangladesh. If Bangladesh improves worker safety, corporations threaten to move somewhere else or simply sue the crap out of an impoverished government.

The result has been, over the past forty-plus years, the closing of over seventy thousand American manufacturing establishments and the transfer of tens of millions of well-paying, mostly unionized, American jobs to Mexico, China, Vietnam, and elsewhere.

The transformation brought about by neoliberal Reaganomics was epitomized by GE CEO Jack Welch, who famously argued that factories shouldn't be tied to any particular country, so that whenever cheaper labor became available across the horizon, one should simply be able to float to set up in that new location.

"Ideally," went his famous and oft-quoted mantra, "you'd have every plant you own on a barge."

The result is that workers across the poorer countries of the world are trapped in a bidding war against each other, each nation offering worse conditions to attract corporate investments. The widespread middle class that took root in America, then Europe and Japan after World War II, is being systematically prevented from emerging in developing nations.

Although they love to call it free trade, it isn't by a long shot. Instead, it's a system designed to keep labor cheap, pollution easy, and corporate profits high. It's the globalization of the oligarch's century-long war against the American Dream.

NAFTA and Investor Rights

The North American Free Trade Agreement, which took effect in 1994, contained a bizarre provision that triggered alarm bells among democracy advocates around the planet: chapter 11, the so-called investor–state dispute settlement mechanism.

Chapter 11 allowed corporations to sue governments in private tribunals set up by those very corporations whenever regulations hurt their profits. These weren't regular courts, where democratic accountability and transparency exist: instead, they're private tribunals run by corporate lawyers, that are shrouded in secrecy and thus shielded from public scrutiny.

The cases were predictable:

A Canadian company sued Mexico for refusing a permit for a toxic waste facility that would have poisoned both air and water, claiming this violated their investment rights. They won $16 million.

An American company sued Canada for banning a cancer-causing gasoline additive that contaminated groundwater, claiming this violated their property rights. Canada paid $13 million to settle.

A timber company sued Canada for putting into law sustainable forestry regulations, claiming lost profits because they couldn't clear-cut and leave the land a wreck. They won $122 million.

These were not trade disputes. These cases—and there are hundreds more—were simple examples of corporations using treaty law to assert the equivalent of American corporate constitutional rights and its claimed "corporate constitutional rights" to override democratically passed environmental protections, public health measures, and local governance.

This is corporate constitutional rights gone global, with transnational corporations (typically based in America) claiming treaty rights that trump democracy.

And remember what Ross Perot warned about during the 1992

presidential election: NAFTA would create a "giant sucking sound" of jobs leaving America. He was, of course, right. The Economic Policy Institute estimates that just NAFTA alone cost the United States nearly seven hundred thousand manufacturing jobs as, in its early years, production moved to Mexico. Most were the very same good jobs that had first built and sustained the American middle class.

Canada became the most frequently sued party under NAFTA's chapter 11, facing thirty-five investor–state disputes over the agreement's lifetime. It lost or settled multiple cases and paid out over $200 million to American investors. The United States, by contrast, never lost a single NAFTA dispute: the system worked exactly as America's corporate oligarchs designed it, resting on the foundation of Davis's headnote.

From NAFTA to USMCA: A Partial Retreat

In July 2020, NAFTA was replaced by the United States–Mexico–Canada Agreement, or USMCA. This new agreement contained what, at first, appeared to be a significant rollback of corporate power: the investor–state dispute settlement mechanism was dramatically dialed back at the insistence of Canada and Mexico. Trump was desperate for a win with the election coming, so he went along with it.

Canada withdrew from investor–state arbitration entirely and, as of July 2023, American and Canadian investors can no longer sue each other's governments in private tribunals. They instead must use regular courts, just like before NAFTA first went into effect.

This is progress. It shows that grassroots efforts and a less-wealthy nation's opposition to corporate power can win real victories.

But the USMCA still contains significant investor protections that are now mostly sector-specific. American corporations operating in Mexico's oil and gas, power generation, telecommunications, transportation, and infrastructure sectors can still use the full investor–state mechanism to force their way. And similar provisions remain embedded in hundreds of other trade and investment agreements written by corporate lawyers and passed by governments beholden to corporate and oligarch money all around the world.

The template that NAFTA created—corporations asserting their human rights to sue governments just for governing on behalf of their people or environment—has spread globally in a mere thirty-plus years. Since 1993, multinational corporations have brought over a thousand investor–state cases worldwide, demanding hundreds of billions of dollars from governments that dared protect their citizens and lands.

The TPP: What We Stopped

Obama's Trans-Pacific Partnership, negotiated in secret by corporate lobbyists and bought-off government officials, would have extended corporate rights to twelve Pacific Rim nations, representing 40 percent of global GDP.

The TPP's investor–state dispute provisions would have allowed corporations to sue governments for regulations that reduced expected future profits, challenge and strike down environmental laws, gut labor protections, outlaw consumer safety regulations, and freely override local democratic decisions in the venues of these private tribunals.

Leaked documents revealed to a shocked world that corporate lawyers had maintained extraordinary and secret control over the negotiations while elected representatives and the public were effectively shut out; even the mainstream media picked up the story.

As a result, the TPP failed, almost entirely because of grassroots opposition from Americans who understood it as a corporate power grab, a victory that proved it's still possible for organized citizens to defeat organized money.

But similar agreements persist, and new ones like these are being negotiated every day, all grounded in the notion of corporate "rights." The TPP was just a short-term setback; the oligarch's battle to establish corporate globalization continues ahead under full steam.

Exporting the Destruction of the American Dream

America's industrial and tech oligarchs didn't just attack the American Dream at home to jack up their profits and riches; they gleefully exported its destruction to the rest of the world.

Between 1980 and today, for example, the United States lost over 6 million manufacturing jobs. The sector that employed nearly 20 million workers at its peak now only employs around 12.7 million, and most pay a fraction (inflation adjusted) of what they did when Reagan took office. Many of those jobs went to countries such as China and Mexico, where wages were a fraction of American wages and environmental and labor regulations were weak or nonexistent.

But when those jobs moved overseas, they didn't create an American Dream in China, Vietnam, or Mexico. Instead, they let mostly American corporations set up sweatshops, increase pollution, and jump into a race to the bottom that keeps wages low everywhere.

The oligarchs successfully played workers in multiple different countries against each other, just as GE's Jack Welch envisioned. American workers were told they had to accept lower wages and a loss of union rights, or their jobs would be shipped to Mexican workers. Mexican workers were told they had to accept poverty wages or lose their livelihoods to Chinese workers. Chinese workers were told they must accept brutal conditions or lose their jobs to Vietnamese workers.

On top of that, as Adam Smith pointed out in *Wealth of Nations*, countries can only generate national wealth by growing things, mining or harvesting things, or manufacturing things. When manufacturing goes overseas, the wealth being created by America goes with it. In part, that explains the post-Reagan collapse of the middle class.

Everyone lost with these trade deals except the morbidly rich CEOs, shareholders, and senior executives of America's largest corporations (and their attorneys), who kept telling us during the 1990s and early 2000s that more cheap goods from overseas would enhance the lifestyle of average Americans.

Turns out, it was a vicious lie.

The Center for Economic and Policy Research found that trade-related wage losses outweighed the gains from cheaper goods for the vast majority of American workers. Workers without college degrees make up 58 percent of the US workforce and have lost more than 12 percent of their wages just under NAFTA-style trade agreements, even after accounting for the "benefits" of cheaper goods.

This isn't an accident or some sort of temporary and unintended aberration; it's the system working exactly as designed by corporate lawyers who base their claim to corporate rights on Davis's phony headnote.

The Rise of Global Oligarchy

As a result of this worldwide spread of corporate constitutional rights, Davis's headnote has created a new global oligarchy that's replaced the kings and queens of old. A new class of ultra-wealthy individuals now controls massive corporations that would have dwarfed the East India Company, buys and sells governments, and regularly operates above—and often simply ignores—national, state, and local law.

The numbers are staggering, as Oxfam points out. The collective wealth of the world's billionaires reached $15 trillion in 2024, up from $13 trillion the year before, a $2 trillion increase that amounted to roughly $5.7 billion per day. The wealth of the richest ten individuals grew in that one year by almost $100 million a day.[46]

There are, as of this 2025 writing, 2,769 billionaires worldwide. At the current rates, Oxfam predicts our world will have five trillionaires within a decade, each controlling unimaginable economic and political power. Elon Musk alone—without whom, Donald Trump may well have not been elected to a second term—is on track to become the world's first trillionaire by 2027, if not sooner.

Perhaps most revealing is the stunning fact that 60 percent of American billionaires' wealth is now unearned, coming instead from inheritance, monopoly power, or crony connections to governments. Every American billionaire under thirty has inherited their wealth, including the new rightwing owner of America's premiere movie and news operations including CBS. For the first time ever, more new billionaires got rich through inheritance than through entrepreneurship or invention. Call it the Lucky Sperm Club.

As much as they try to convince us that we're seeing the rise of self-made geniuses, the reality is that today we're confronted by the emergence of a new and toxic hereditary aristocracy that dwarfs the days of trustbuster Teddy Roosevelt, an oligarchic class that passes wealth and power from generation to generation without meaningful taxation, all as the rest of America struggles to stay afloat.

Meanwhile, the number of Americans living in poverty has barely changed since 1990. The richest 1 percent owns fully 43 percent of all global financial assets. The top 10 percent take more than half of all income. The system extracts $30 million per hour from the bottom 90 percent of the Global South and sends it to the richest 1 percent in the United States.[47]

As Oxfam's executive director put it: "The capture of our global economy by a privileged few has reached heights once considered unimaginable."

The Oligarch International

Today's new breed of morbidly rich oligarchs and their corporations operate above and beyond national boundaries. The three richest in America—Bezos, Musk, and Zuckerberg—are clear examples.

Jeff Bezos can move his Amazon operations to whichever country offers the best tax deal, bust unions with enthusiasm, and sanitize it all with his ownership of *The Washington Post*. His apparent loyalty is to making money, not to any nation or community.

Elon Musk can manipulate stock markets, ignore labor laws, use his riches and his social media platform to help friendly politicians, and thumb his nose at regulations because he has enough wealth to fight legal battles indefinitely. In exchange for the quarter-billion-dollar "campaign contribution" he gave to get Trump elected, that administration gave him the power to shut down or kneecap over twenty agencies that had been investigating his business practices, saving him *billions* in legal costs and fines. His massive fortune gives him more economic power than most nations.

Mark Zuckerberg controls a communications platform used by billions, decides what speech is allowed and what is banned or shadow-banned, and also faces minimal democratic accountability.

Billionaires now run or are the principal shareholders of more than a third of the world's top fifty corporations. The total market capitalization of these corporations is over $13 trillion. Three American asset managers alone—BlackRock, State Street, and Vanguard—hold $20 trillion in assets, close to one-fifth of all investable assets in the world, and all three claim corporate constitutional rights.[48]

These are not aberrations. They're the intentional, constructed features of a global system where oligarchs use corporate power derived from corporate "rights" to escape democratic control by We the People.

They owe loyalty to nothing except their own wealth and power, much like the railroad oligarchs of the twenty-first century, only now operating at global scale.

The Climate Connection

Corporate power is also why America is failing to meaningfully address climate change, which kills thousands of us every year and is increasingly pushing our planet toward uninhabitability.

Fossil fuel corporations and their executives have known since the 1970s that their products would cause catastrophic climate change if they weren't held in check or replaced by green alternatives. They thus had two choices: transition to clean energy or lie, which includes funding climate change denial and blocking government action.

To maintain their profits, they chose lies and obstruction.

ExxonMobil, Shell, BP, and other oil giants spent billions funding climate change denial, lobbying against climate legislation, and using their corporate constitutional rights to buy politicians and judges while fighting regulations.

When states tried to investigate whether ExxonMobil had committed fraud by hiding its own researcher's climate science from the public, the corporation claimed First Amendment free speech rights (the Supreme Court has ruled that "the right to refuse to speak" is as much a free speech right as "the right to speak") protecting them from investigation.

As a result, when governments try to regulate carbon emissions, corporations sue, claiming "regulatory takings" violates their Fourteenth and Fifth Amendment property rights.

Corporate constitutional rights gave fossil fuel oligarchs the weapons they're now enthusiastically wielding to sacrifice human civilization for quarterly profits.

This isn't hyperbole. The science is clear: without rapid decarbonization, we face the potential of civilizational collapse within this century, and corporate power is the primary obstacle to the action we need.

The stakes today aren't just democratic: they're existential.

The Solution Must Be Global

Fighting corporate constitutional rights in America is essential, but it won't be sufficient in this brave new world. The planet needs a global movement to reassert democratic control over corporations. This means

† Ending investor–state dispute provisions in all trade agreements. Corporations should never be able to sue governments for simply governing on behalf of their citizens.

† Creating international corporate taxation systems that prevent profit-shifting and tax avoidance. Corporations should pay taxes wherever they do business, not, like today, just where they hide their profits.

† Establishing enforceable global environmental standards that corporations can't escape by cynically moving operations from one country to another.

† Protecting and normalizing labor rights internationally so corporations can no longer create and then exploit a race to the bottom in wages and working conditions.

† Breaking up multinational and domestic monopolies so no corporation is too big to fail or too big to regulate.

† And most fundamentally, rejecting the premise that corporations have rights that trump democratic governance anywhere in the world.

This is a massive undertaking, but one that's absolutely necessary. Corporate power doesn't respect borders, which is why neither can our resistance.

The American Leadership Role

America exported Davis's fraudulent corporate constitutional rights to the world. America, therefore, has both a moral and legal responsibility to help undo the damage.

By passing a constitutional amendment ending corporate constitutional rights, America would prove that democracy can defeat oligarchy, establish a viable model for other nations, eliminate American support for global investor–state systems, and shift the global balance of power toward democratic control of corporations and their oligarchs.

People are largely awake and aware of these issues, even if they can't name them, and the world is watching. If America can undo the crime of corporate constitutional rights, other nations will follow.

On the other hand, if America fails, oligarchy goes global permanently.

And with it, the American Dream will die not just in America but everywhere. The promise that hard work can still bring prosperity, that ordinary people can build prosperous lives for their families, and that democracy can constrain corporate power all vanishes.

Outgoing President Joe Biden, in his farewell address in January 2025, warned of "an oligarchy taking shape in America of extreme wealth, power and influence." He was right. But it wasn't just "taking shape": it arrived with the Reagan Revolution, based on Davis's headnote, and is now in full flower. And it's not just taking an axe to the American Dream; this time it's gone global.

As a result, the stakes couldn't be higher.

17

Corporate Immortality and Unequal Risk

WHEN MARTHA STEWART LIED TO INVESTIGATORS ABOUT A STOCK sale, she was arrested, convicted, fined, and sent to federal prison. On the other hand, when the Pfizer corporation pled guilty to multiple criminal felonies in 2009, marketing drugs illegally in ways that led to multiple patient deaths, the corporation paid $2.3 billion in fines.

Not one of Pfizer's executives, decision makers, or shareholders spent a single night in jail or even personally paid a fine.

This isn't an anomaly or a loophole: it's the system working exactly as the corporate oligarchs designed it to work, premised on corporate constitutional rights resting on the foundation of Davis's headnote.

FDR's American Dream promised that if you worked hard and played by the rules, you could build a secure life for yourself and your family. But the rules since the Reagan Revolution and *Citizens United* are increasingly rigged against us humans: corporations can destroy communities, poison workers, crash the economy, and continue to "live free" while the working people who lose their jobs, their homes, their health, and their futures have little to no recourse.

Corporate constitutional rights created a system where corporations and their senior executives exclusively risk capital while working-class people risk everything else, including their families and their lives.

The Superpower of Immortality

Corporations also possess something no human being has ever had but generations have dreamed of: immortality.

You will die. I will die. Everyone we both know will die. But corporations continue. Unless their charter is revoked, something that almost never happens anymore, corporations can outlive entire generations of humans, accumulating wealth and power across centuries.

The British East India Company existed for 274 years. Modern American corporations plan in similar timeframes: they play long games that no human lifespan can match.

This creates a fundamental asymmetry of power. Humans think in terms of decades; corporations think in terms of centuries. Humans face death as the ultimate accountability; corporations face no such constraint.

When a human commits murder, he or she can be imprisoned or executed. When a corporation commits manslaughter—and corporate manslaughter is legally recognized—the corporation continues operating, perhaps paying a fine that is often tax-deductible.

Union Carbide killed thousands in Bhopal, India, in 1984, when a poorly maintained chemical plant exploded, releasing toxic gas into densely populated neighborhoods. The corporation paid compensation to victims (though far less than was deserved), was bought by Dow Chemical, and continues operating today. Not a single executive went to prison or paid a personal fine, and neither company faced the corporate death penalty of charter revocation.

Tobacco companies knew for decades that their product was both addictive and deadly. They lied about it, marketed to children, and caused millions of preventable deaths including that of my brother, Stanley. After decades of citizen activism, they finally paid fines and legal settlements. But they're still operating, still selling the same deadly product, still making profits, and the men and women who made decisions that today create an estimated half million deaths a year never spent a day in jail.

Banks crashed the global economy in 2008 through fraudulent mortgage securities and reckless speculation. Millions lost jobs, homes, and savings. The banks got bailouts and then emerged bigger than before. Not a single major bank lost its charter and not a single CEO went to prison for the frauds that destroyed countless lives; to the contrary, many walked away with millions and even billions in bonuses and other compensation.

The pattern is consistent: corporations and their executives when operating behind the corporate shield can commit crimes that would land average humans in prison for decades or even life, and they face no comparable consequences.

The Corporate Veil

This immunity was not always the norm. In America's early years, corporate shareholders could be held personally liable for corporate harms.

If you invested in a corporation that poisoned a river, you could lose your house to pay damages. If your company's negligence killed workers, you could face personal legal consequences. If your corporation committed fraud, you could go to jail.

Then came the widespread adoption of "limited liability," the legal innovation Queen Elizabeth I first proposed in 1601 that built a wall between corporate actions and shareholder responsibility.

The logic seemed reasonable: encourage investment by limiting investor risk to the amount invested. If you buy $1,000 in stock, you can lose that $1,000, but you won't lose your house if the corporation does something terrible.

The result was predictable: it encouraged terrible behavior by eliminating personal accountability.

Today, if you invest in a corporation that commits environmental devastation, labor exploitation, or even manslaughter, your maximum loss is your stock value. You will not face criminal prosecution, face personal lawsuits, or lose anything except your investment (unless you're running a small, one-person company).

The modern stock corporation has become a perfect liability shield for America's oligarchs to extract profits while dumping all the risk on everyone else.

When BP's Deepwater Horizon oil rig exploded in 2010, killing eleven workers and causing the largest marine oil spill in history, BP's shareholders didn't lose their houses and their executives didn't go to jail. They lost some stock value for a short time, but that was it.

When pharmaceutical companies sold opioids that they knew were addictive—triggering an epidemic—the executives made fortunes. The Sackler family, who owned Purdue Pharma and knowingly facilitated these deaths, extracted billions before the company declared bankruptcy. They kept most of their wealth and nobody spent a single day in jail.

The corporate veil, resting on the foundation of corporate constitutional rights, routinely protects oligarchs from the often-deadly consequences of their own greed.

The Redistribution of Risk

As you can see, modern corporate constitutional rights didn't just grant corporations rights; they fundamentally offloaded risk onto the rest of society.

Before corporate constitutional rights, corporations bore most of the risk of their activities. If they poisoned a river, they paid to clean it up. If they hurt workers, they paid compensation. If they defrauded customers, they faced penalties that could destroy the corporation.

After corporations were granted constitutional rights, the risk equation reversed. Corporations risk capital—the money (often other people's money) invested in the business—but humans risk everything else: health, safety, environment, community, democracy, and ultimately survival.

A chemical company risks quarterly profits. Nearby residents risk cancer from toxic exposure.

A pharmaceutical company risks market share and stock price. Patients risk death or disability from untested or deceptively marketed drugs rushed to market.

A fossil fuel company risks somewhat lower returns. Everyone on Earth risks climate catastrophe.

This is not an equal exchange: it is, instead, a parasitic form of wealth extraction from society. Oligarchs extract their profits while exporting the real risks to the rest of us.

And corporate constitutional rights protect this arrangement. When communities try to protect themselves from corporate harm, corporations sue, claiming their rights are being violated. Under the Constitution designed for people, they now have Fourteenth Amendment due process rights, Fifth Amendment property rights, First Amendment rights to advertise harmful products, and even Fourth and Fifth Amendment privacy rights against "unreasonable" inspections or having to tell the truth about what they're up to. All because of Davis's corrupt headnote.

Every constitutional right claimed by corporations today has become a weapon they can use to prevent democratic governmental protections for the rest of us from their corporate harm.

The American Dream Reversed

The entire premise of FDR's twentieth-century American Dream promised that our hard work would be rewarded, that taking modest risks like starting a small business could pay off, and that if you played by the rules, you could build a comfortable future for your family.

Corporate constitutional rights reversed all of it.

Today, thanks to corporate constitutional rights, corporations bank their profits while we suffer the risks to our health, our local communities, our planet's atmosphere, and to our children's and grandchildren's futures.

Consider the simple example of what happens when a corporation decides to exploit one of the neoliberal trade agreements to close a factory and move its operations overseas.

The corporation essentially risks nothing. If the overseas operation fails, they can move again, or restructure, or even declare bankruptcy and start afresh. The senior executives keep their bonuses, the shareholders keep their dividends, and the corporation rolls along in a new location.

The workers, however, risked everything. They lost their jobs, their health insurance, and many lose their homes when they can't find new work. History shows that many will lose their marriages under the stress of unemployment. Their families are crushed as they watch their children's opportunities shrink while the rich get richer by the day.

The community where the corporation operates also risks pretty much everything when companies go off in search of cheaper labor or laxer environmental or labor regulations. The local tax base collapses, schools lose funding, roads deteriorate, and local businesses that depended on the factory workers close. Young people begin to leave in search of opportunities elsewhere as their once-vibrant community hollows out and dies.

This happened in hundreds of American towns when corporations first began to seriously exploit the constitutional rights Davis and Field set up for them between the neoliberal Reagan Revolution of the 1980s and today—in the Rust Belt, Appalachian coal country, textile towns across the South, Detroit, and Flint, Michigan. Communities that had built middle-class prosperity over generations were shattered in a decade or two because corporations faced no consequences for abandoning them.

Corporate constitutional rights gave giant corporations the rights they wanted to make these decisions without accountability. They can now claim their property rights, their freedom of contract, their due process protections, even the right to hide their own crimes and knowledge of dangerous products, while citizens and communities have essentially no recourse.

The American Dream didn't just begin to fade with the Reagan Revolution: it was stripped away, community by community, family by family, worker by worker, all by corporations that faced no consequences for the devastation they left behind.

Wage Theft and Worker Exploitation

Every year, corporations steal more from workers through wage theft than all the burglaries, robberies, and car thefts in America *combined*.

The Economic Policy Institute estimates that workers collectively lose over $50 billion every year to wage theft: unpaid overtime, minimum wage violations, illegal deductions, and forced off-the-clock work.[49]

When a person robs a convenience store for $200, they're arrested and can go to prison. When a corporation steals $200 million from its workers, it just pays a fine (if it's caught at all) and continues operating. And not a single executive ever spends a night in jail.

Walmart alone has paid hundreds of millions in wage theft settlements, yet remains America's largest employer.[50] The executives who oversaw the theft kept their jobs and bonuses. The corporation's charter was never threatened. And, of course, this isn't limited to Walmart.

This nightmare has become, in the wake of the Reagan Revolution and its reliance on Davis's corporate constitutional rights, the American Dream in reverse. Workers who play by the rules, who show up on time, who work hard have their wages stolen by corporations that face no meaningful consequences.

And when workers try to fight back, corporations invariably invoke their constitutional rights. They force workers into mandatory arbitration, using their constitutional freedom of contract rights to strip workers of their Seventh Amendment right to a jury trial. They use their First Amendment free speech rights to run anti-union campaigns. They claim their Fifth Amendment property rights are violated by labor regulations.

The same constitutional rights that were put into law by our Founders to protect human beings from government tyranny now protect corporations from accountability for stealing from or otherwise damaging or even killing their workers.

The Precautionary Principle

Most democratic nations today use something called the "precautionary principle": if you want to release a new chemical, drug, or technology into society, you must first prove that it's safe.

The entire burden of proof is on the corporation to demonstrate safety before being allowed to sell, which just makes sense, right? Better safe than sorry. Don't release new products until you know they won't hurt people.

America—alone among developed countries in the world—does the opposite. We use what's sometimes called the "reactionary principle": corporations can release products and they stay in the marketplace, environment, or even food supply until someone proves they're dangerous.

By the time proof of harm emerges, of course, people are already sick or even dead. Communities are already poisoned. Ecosystems are already damaged. And the corporation and its senior executives and shareholders have already made their billions in profits.

Why does America reject the precautionary principle? Because corporate constitutional rights gave corporations the same due process rights as human beings and the free speech rights to buy politicians and regulators.

Their lawyers tell us (and Republicans on the Supreme Court back them up) that we can't ban a product without proof it is harmful: that would violate Fifth Amendment corporate property rights and Fourteenth Amendment due process rights. The burden of proof shifted from corporations (prove your product is safe) to victims (prove the product harmed you).

This shift has been deadly for Americans (and much of the rest of the world that doesn't have strong regulations but purchases US-made chemicals, additives, and products).

The CDC estimates that over 80,000 chemicals are currently in commercial use in America. Most have never been properly tested for human health effects, and new chemicals are introduced daily.

As a result, we and our children are living through a massive, uncontrolled experiment. We're the test subjects, even though none of us ever gave our consent.

Corporations release chemicals into our bodies, our water, our air, and our food. When those chemicals turn out to cause cancer, birth defects, or neurological damage, the burden falls to us victims to prove it. But by then, the damage is done and the billionaires have already banked their profits.

Meanwhile, corporations have Fifth Amendment rights against self-incrimination so they can hide their own internal studies showing their products are dangerous, suppress evidence of potential harms, and even seal court settlements to prevent the public from ever learning the truth.

In 1950 my mom got pregnant with me, so my dad dropped out of college to take a job in a steel factory, where the hot steel came out of the blast furnace over asbestos-covered rollers. The company that made those rollers had known for at least fifteen years that their product caused mesothelioma, the wildly painful and always-fatal form of lung cancer that killed my father.

My little brother Stanley started smoking when we were teenagers and kept it up most of his life. When we were kids, Ronald Reagan was doing TV ads for Chesterfield cigarettes, wearing a doctor's white coat and assuring us most doctors smoked that brand. I loved Stan dearly, and knowing he died gasping for breath haunts me—and enrages me—to this day.

But even then, the asbestos and tobacco corporations were claiming a Fifth Amendment right to hide what they knew.

The constitutional rights our Founders fought and died for, meant to protect innocent humans from government tyranny, now instead protect guilty corporations from accountability.

The Numbers Don't Lie

Corporate America has killed more Americans than all our foreign wars *combined.*

Tobacco alone kills an estimated 480,000 Americans every year. That's more than World War I, World War II, Korea, Vietnam, Iraq, and Afghanistan combined, and it happens every single year.[51]

The opioid epidemic has killed over 806,000 Americans since 1999, fueled by pharmaceutical executives who knew their products were addictive and lied about it.[52]

Workplace injuries and occupational diseases kill approximately 120,000 Americans annually.[53]

Air pollution from corporate sources kills an estimated 100,000 Americans every year.[54]

These are *not* accidents or simply the cost of having a vibrant economy, as corporate shill economists like to claim. Instead, they're the predictable results of a system that prioritizes corporate profits over human lives, enabled by corporate constitutional rights that shield corporations from accountability.

No CEO has ever been executed for these deaths, although if you'd done any of this yourself in a state with capital punishment, you'd be long gone. No CEO has ever been imprisoned or forced to attend the funerals of the people killed by their business choices. Most have never been meaningfully punished in any way whatsoever.

If a human killed 480,000 people every year, we'd call them the worst mass murderer in history. When corporations routinely do it, year after year for decades, we call it "business."

The Deepwater Horizon Example

The BP Deepwater Horizon disaster in 2010 illustrates everything that's wrong with this form of immunity that comes from the weapon Davis's headnote gave corrupt Republicans on the Supreme Court to grant corporations human rights.

BP's well blowout killed eleven workers and spilled 4.9 million barrels of oil into the Gulf of Mexico, and news organizations and courts explicitly found it was caused by BP's systematic cost cutting, senior executives intentionally ignoring safety warnings, and reckless risk taking from well management all the way up to the boardroom.

BP pled guilty to eleven counts of manslaughter, one count of lying to Congress, and multiple violations of the Clean Water Act and the Migratory Bird Treaty Act. They paid $4.5 billion in fines and settlements.

That's a pile of cash to you or me, and sounds like accountability, at least until you look deeper.

BP's revenue in 2010 was $308 billion. The fines thus represented less than 2 percent of annual revenue.

And to really push our faces in it, BP took tax deductions for much of the settlement, meaning Gulf Coast taxpayers subsidized their own compensation.

No BP executive was imprisoned for the eleven manslaughter counts, and BP continues operating as one of the world's largest corporations.

There was also Cameron International, a contractor involved in the disaster: they paid $250 million. Halliburton paid $1.1 billion. Transocean paid $1.4 billion.

Spread the blame, spread the costs, ensure no single corporation faces crippling consequences. And none of the executives from those companies went to jail, either.

This is how personhood's corporate immunity works. Massive harm, modest fines, no charter revocation, no criminal prosecution of the decision makers, and continued operation.

If those eleven humans had been murdered by a deranged person, the killer would face life in prison or even execution. When a corporation commits manslaughter eleven times through reckless cost cutting, however, it pays a fine smaller than annual marketing budgets and is then reimbursed by us taxpayers through tax deductibility.

Corporate Death Became Virtually Impossible

In the early American republic, states regularly revoked corporate charters when corporations violated the public trust. It was called the "corporate death penalty," and it was used frequently.

If a corporation polluted a river, defrauded customers, or otherwise harmed the community, the state could simply end its existence, and it was gone.

Then the early doctrine of corporate constitutional rights changed everything in the late nineteenth and early twentieth centuries. Once corporations gained constitutional rights, particularly due process rights under the Fourteenth Amendment, states could no longer easily revoke charters.

Revocation of a company's charter became a Fifth Amendment "taking" of the "corporate person's" property without due process. It required lengthy legal proceedings. Corporations could afford unlimited legal bills to fight revocation, but the costs became prohibitive for states in the tight post-Reagan tax-cut era.

Corporate death penalties, as a result, have become virtually impossible.

Even after massive crimes, environmental devastation, fraudulent bankruptcies, and systematic law breaking, including the killing of hundreds of thousands of Americans, corporations survive. They might be restructured, rebranded, or bought by other corporations, but they persist.

"Too big to fail" has become "too criminal to punish": the bigger and more connected a corporation is and the more politicians it's purchased using Clarence Thomas's *Citizens United* decision, the less likely it is that it'll ever face real consequences.

This is, again, no mistake; it's intentional and has been since the days of Davis and Field. Using this clearly absurd argument that corporations are entitled to human rights found in the Constitution, corporate oligarchs designed and have fine-tuned a system where their companies and executives can commit crimes with near-total impunity.

The Promise Betrayed

The American Dream was built on a simple promise: work hard, play by the rules, and you can build a good life for yourself and your family.

Corporate constitutional rights have violently betrayed that promise.

It's created a two-tiered system where corporations play by an entirely different set of rules than humans, even though it's all grounded in what were intended to be *human* rights in the first place. Corporations can poison, steal, and kill with minimal consequences; and when the gains from productivity and technology arrive, they invariably flow upward to CEO oligarchs while the risks trickle down to workers and their communities.

In 1980, when a single income could support a family, and two-thirds of Americans were middle class, the system still worked for most people. Corporations and their executives had power, but so did workers, through their unions; and communities, through their elected governments.

Then Reagan took office and embraced Lewis Powell's *Memo* and his decision in *Bellotti,* making corporate constitutional rights into weapons that began to destroy everything that made the American Dream possible.[55]

The American middle class isn't dying of natural causes. It's being killed, deliberately and systematically, by corporations wielding constitutional rights that were meant for human beings.

And until we undo that fundamental crime, until we strip corporations of constitutional rights and restore democratic control over these artificial entities, the killing will continue.

18

The Media Oligopoly

In 1983, FULLY FIFTY CORPORATIONS CONTROLLED MOST MAJOR American media: television, radio, newspapers, magazines, books, and film. Today, that number is six, and soon it might be three.

This isn't market consolidation; it's the strangulation of democracy following a model pioneered by Vladamir Putin and Viktor Orbán, and championed by Ronald Reagan and Donald Trump. And it wouldn't have been possible without corporate constitutional rights.

This is crucial because media consolidation doesn't just threaten democracy in the abstract. It hides, instead, the very story of how the American Dream was stolen by these parasites. It suppresses coverage of the solutions that could bring it back.

It ensures that most Americans never discover why their wages stagnated, why their healthcarc costs have exploded, or why their children face crushing debt for the same college education that was free or nearly free when my generation was coming up.

Today's morbidly rich corporate oligarchs don't just control the economy: they control the story that we tell ourselves about the economy. And that control is worth more than all their other investments combined.

The First Amendment Theft

The First Amendment is explicit: "Congress shall make no law…abridging the freedom of speech, or of the press."

Those words were written to protect human beings like you and me. They were designed for pamphleteers like Thomas Paine, who printed *Common Sense* in his workshop and changed history. Newspaper editors once could criticize government without fear of prosecution, being publicly targeted for death threats, or lawsuits and other harassment by the Trump administration. It was explicitly written so American citizens could forever speak truth to power without fear.

The Founders had both seen press censorship in Britain and experienced it in the colonies. They wrote the First Amendment to ensure that human beings could communicate freely, especially about political matters. Empowering reporters, newspapers, and other public media to hold government to account was so vital to the Framers of the Constitution that they wrote it into the very first of the Bill of Rights' ten amendments.

They never imagined it would be perverted by an on-the-take court reporter and, later, five corrupt Republicans on the Supreme Court to give oligarch-owned corporations unlimited power to buy elections and dominate the content of everything from news to social media and the results coming from search engines and AI.

But that's exactly what happened, through corporate constitutional rights.

The Path from Press Freedom to Corporate Dominance

For most of American history, the First Amendment meant what it said: protection for human speech and for the press as an institution.

The "press" in 1791—when the First Amendment was ratified—meant *printing presses*, the physical tools that individuals and small groups used to publish pamphlets, newspapers, and books. Towns often had multiple newspapers representing different viewpoints, and any citizen with modest means could start a newspaper, as Alexis de Tocqueville pointed out in amazement in his 1835 book *Democracy in America*: the "marketplace of ideas" was actually a marketplace.

Even into the mid-twentieth century—largely as a result of legislation passed in the 1920s as radio was becoming a thing—media ownership was relatively dispersed. Cities had competing newspapers. Radio stations were locally owned. Television was dominated by three networks, but they faced strict fairness and equal-time regulations.

Then two things changed: media consolidation and corporate First Amendment rights.

The first enabled concentration of ownership. The second blocked democratic attempts to stop it.

The Media Consolidation Timeline

While *Citizens United* opened unlimited corporate money in politics with most of it spent on television and other advertising, other developments had already enabled unprecedented media consolidation:

In the 1980s, Reagan's FCC begins eliminating ownership limits; one company can now own multiple stations in the same market. Reagan also fast-tracked the US citizenship of Rupert Murdoch so he could own TV stations. Reagan then ended enforcement of the Fairness Doctrine and the Equal Time Rule.

In 1996, the Telecommunications Act removed most remaining ownership restrictions and carved out a special "no prosecution, no accountability" for social media with its Section 230 provisions. Media consolidation accelerated dramatically that decade as the programming of over a thousand radio stations flipped rightwing, and about five hundred of them were anchored by Rush Limbaugh.

In the 2000s, the internet devastated local newspapers. Google and Facebook monopolized digital advertising and refused to publicly disclose their algorithms. Local journalism collapsed at the same time that half of America's local newspapers became the property of new giant corporations that began to dictate both news and editorial content.

From 2010 to today, streaming services and tech giants have dominated, and six corporations now control most American media.

At each stage, when government tried to maintain ownership limits or enforce diversity-of-opinion requirements, corporations sued, claiming First Amendment violations. Courts, following the *Bellotti* and *Citizens United* logic, typically sided with the corporations.

Corporate First Amendment rights thus destroyed virtually every democratic safeguard against media monopoly.

The Six Corporations

Comcast, The Walt Disney Company, Paramount Skydance, Warner Bros. Discovery, Fox Corporation, and Sony Pictures Entertainment—these six sprawling conglomerates still dominate most of America's national media as of January 2026, and two are openly controlled by rightwing billionaires.

This tiny group controls most of the major television networks, many of the most-watched cable channels, the bulk of America's major film studios, and most of the major streaming platforms. They influence what movies get made, what shows get promoted, what news gets covered or ignored, and what cultural stories or moral panics reach the public. They own or control large chunks of radio and TV, major music labels, and important parts of the book-publishing world.

And then there's Sinclair Broadcast Group. It isn't one of the Big Six national entertainment conglomerates, but it *is* the single most powerful force in local broadcast news. With over 185 stations reaching roughly 40 percent of American households, Sinclair controls and distributes the nightly local news many Americans trust most.[56] Through centralized "must-run" segments and coordinated editorial directives, Sinclair's management shapes political messaging at the community level in ways the national giants never could.

Together, these companies—backed by and intertwined with massive institutional investors like BlackRock, Vanguard, and State Street—determine what most Americans watch, hear, and read. They decide which parts of the news get told, which issues get covered, and whose versions of reality are available to us.

The Illusion of Choice

Walk down a grocery aisle. You'll see a hundred brands of cereal, fifty brands of chips, thirty brands of soda. It looks like an abundance of choice, all presumably benefitting us consumers because of competition.

But look behind all those brand names and you'll discover that ten corporations own almost everything that's sold in supermarkets today.

And those ten corporations are largely owned by the same groups of institutional investors.

Media works the same way: hundreds of stations and channels, thousands of shows, millions of websites. It looks like diversity.

But six corporations control the distribution. The oligarchs control the corporations. And increasingly, the same oligarchs control all six through overlapping ownership.

We're not actually choosing what to watch; instead, we're choosing from what they allow us to watch.

This illusion of choice is far more insidious than the kind of blatant, ham-handed censorship that we've seen on Fox "News" for years and is now showing up on CBS. At least with censorship, you know you're being controlled, but with this new form of manufactured choice, you think you're free while morbidly rich oligarchs are managing every option on the menu.

Hiding the Death of the American Dream

This is a massive issue and crisis for America: corporate media consolidation doesn't just threaten democracy; it also hides the very story of what happened to FDR's American Dream.

When was the last time you saw in-depth coverage on network television about why wages have stagnated for forty-five years while productivity and corporate profits soared? Or how about how that $50 trillion was transferred from working Americans to the top 1 percent between 1975 and 2018?

When was the last time cable news spent an hour examining how corporate constitutional rights enables oligarchic control of our economy and politics, or the ways Putin and Orbán sued their way to near-complete media control in Russia and Hungary, and Trump is doing today?

When was the last time a major newspaper ran a front-page series on how the Reagan Revolution began the systematic dismantling of virtually every policy that built the middle class?

You haven't seen these stories because the corporations that would have to tell them are among the very same corporations that benefit from keeping them hidden.

The death of the American Dream at the hands of corporate constitutional rights is the biggest story of our lifetimes. Two-thirds of Americans lived middle-class lives in 1980, but today it's 43–47 percent. That's tens of millions of families who've lost what their parents and grandparents had and what they'd been promised.

But you'll never see this story told comprehensively on corporate media, because telling it would require explaining who killed the American Dream. And the killers own, in addition to most other American business, the media.

The Stories They Won't Tell

Consider the stories that corporate media systematically ignores, downplays, or frames to protect oligarchic interests.

Union Organizing

When workers try to organize for better wages and conditions, corporate media either ignores it or frames it as disruption and inconvenience. The Amazon warehouse workers trying to unionize? A minor story. The Starbucks baristas organizing across the country? Barely covered. The historic wave of union organizing sweeping America? You'd hardly know it from watching network news.

Why? Because the corporations that own the media don't want their own workers getting ideas. And because their advertisers, other major corporations themselves, also don't want positive coverage of unions.

Living Wages

The Fight for $15 movement helped push minimum wage increases in cities and states across America. But corporate media coverage consistently emphasized business concerns about costs instead of workers' concerns about survival. When workers say they can't afford rent on today's federal minimum wage, that's a "human interest" story, buried in the back pages. When business owners say higher wages might hurt profits, however, that's front-page "economic news."

Medicare for All

Polls consistently show that a majority of Americans support some variation of Medicare for All, a single-payer healthcare system that would eliminate the parasitic insurance industry's control of our healthcare. But corporate media coverage of Medicare for All has been overwhelmingly negative, emphasizing cost concerns while ignoring the studies showing that overall, it would save money for both the nation and individual families. Why? Because insurance companies and pharmaceutical companies are among the biggest advertisers on corporate media, and the networks aren't about to tell you that their sponsors are the reason we all pay roughly twice as much for healthcare as people in all the other developed countries of the world.

Wealth Inequality

Three men own more wealth than the bottom half of Americans combined. That's a staggering fact and reflects a reality we haven't seen since the Gilded Age that led to the Republican Great Depression. It should be headline news every single day until something changes, but, instead, it's just an occasional sidebar, if it's mentioned at all. Corporate media fawningly celebrates billionaires' philanthropy while ignoring how they accumulated that wealth in the first place, exploiting the very policies that destroyed the middle class.

Corporate Crime

When a corporation commits fraud that costs workers their pensions, it's just a footnote in the business news section. When a person robs a convenience store, though, it's front-page crime news with a mugshot.

The framing itself protects the powerful, as corporate crime is normalized, while human crime is sensationalized and exploited for political purposes.

Tax Avoidance

Major corporations and their billionaire oligarchs pay little or no federal income tax as a result of thousands of legal loopholes inserted in our tax code by politicians legally bribed by oligarchs using *Citizens United*. This is reported occasionally, then forgotten. There's never the kind of sustained coverage the subject deserves, which could incite demands for change. You'll never see an investigative series naming the specific lobbyists who wrote the loopholes, the politicians who put them into law, or the oligarchs who get a new yacht because of them.

These aren't random omissions in our information stream: they're systemic. The stories that would help Americans understand why the American Dream has been crushed are precisely the stories that our monopolistic and billionaire-owned corporate media won't tell.

The News Problem

The original purpose of First Amendment press freedom was to enable democratic self-governance. Thomas Jefferson famously said that if he had to choose between government without newspapers or newspapers without government, he'd choose newspapers without government.

Our Founders and the Framers who wrote the Constitution and Bill of Rights believed informed citizens needed access to facts, diverse perspectives, and vigorous debate. A free press, in their minds, was essential to providing those things that would keep our republic functional and free.

But when six corporations control the news, we don't get diversity of opinion or insights into corporate abuse of their newly acquired "human rights." Instead, we get propaganda and milquetoast reporting masquerading as choice and news.

Fox "News" and CNN appear to be opposites, one right-wing, one left-leaning. But both are owned by enormous corporations that benefit from the same things: low corporate taxes, weak regulations, strong intellectual property laws, limited labor rights, and corporate constitutional rights.

Neither questions the fundamental assumptions of corporate capitalism. Neither investigates corporate power deeply. Neither advocates for ending corporate constitutional rights.

Why would they? The corporations that own them benefit from corporate constitutional rights.

The Supreme Court's Complicity

Corporate constitutional rights don't just enable media consolidation: they also actively block "little-guy" attempts to stop it.

The FCC once enforced ownership limits based on the principle that diversity of ownership creates diversity of voices and ideas. One company couldn't own too many stations and newspapers in any one market or state.

Then corporations sued, claiming their First Amendment rights were being violated by ownership restrictions. Courts, accepting that corporations have First Amendment rights because of Davis's headnote, often struck down ownership limits.

The pattern repeated with campaign finance limits, equal-time provisions, and the Fairness Doctrine. Every democratic safeguard against corporate media domination has now fallen before corporate First Amendment claims.

The oligarchs used corporate constitutional rights, created by fraud in 1886, to dismantle every protection we once had against their media monopolies; and in 1996 President Clinton signed the heavily lobbied Telecommunications Act that finally removed from federal law the last meaningful limits on media ownership and consolidation.

What This Means for You

As a result, we all now live in a media environment designed by oligarchs, for the benefit of oligarchs.

The news we watch is filtered through corporate profit motives and oligarchic interests.

The shows we stream were produced by conglomerates that benefit from subtle messages built into stories that validate and strengthen the status quo.

The social media we scroll is controlled by secret algorithms optimized for hate, engagement, and profit—not truth or democracy.

The search results we trust were ranked by a corporation with its own political and economic interests.

Even most of the books we read are published by subsidiaries of or companies associated with the same six media conglomerates.

We think we're making free choices about what information to consume, but we're actually navigating a carefully curated information environment designed to serve oligarchic interests while giving us all the illusion of freedom.

We think we're informed about the world, but we're actually getting a version of the world filtered through corporate priorities.

And the biggest thing they're hiding from us is why our lives are harder than our parents' lives were, why our wages don't go as far, why we can't afford a house, why we're drowning in debt. Why the American Dream died. They're hiding that crime because they themselves benefit from it daily.

The First Amendment Needs Restoration

The Founders never intended that corporations should have First Amendment rights. They never once mentioned corporations in the Constitution. Lewis Powell's assertion in *Bellotti* that a legal fiction created by government charter could have the same free speech rights as a human being would have seemed insane to them.

The solution to this crisis of public information is the same as for all corporate constitutional rights problems: a constitutional amendment clarifying that constitutional rights belong exclusively to human beings.

Once that amendment passes, we can

† Break up media monopolies without corporate First Amendment objections.

† Restore ownership limits to ensure diversity of voices.

† Regulate corporate political spending without claims of censorship.

† Protect human speech without giving oligarchs unlimited amplification through corporate treasuries.

† Revive local journalism through public funding and structural support.

† Restore the First Amendment to its original purpose: protecting human free expression.

Until then, oligarch-owned media corporations will continue to crush human speech under the iron heel of their unlimited "free speech" budgets.

The oligarchs are now working hard to control the past (through censoring our schools and history books), the present (through controlling our news coverage), and the future (by limiting what practical possibilities we can imagine).

This is the endpoint of corporate media consolidation enabled by corporate constitutional rights: totalitarian control of information dressed up as free speech.

And its first casualty is the truth about what happened to the American Dream. From Davis to Powell to Reagan to Trump and his cronies—they stole it. And they're doing their damnest to make sure we never find out how.

But if you've read this book, then you *know* how.

The fight for the American Dream is on.

Join it.

What History Will Say About Us

History teaches us that oligarchies are unstable systems of government that typically either collapse from their own internal rot—as happened here in 1929 when the Republican Great Depression brought down the oligarchs of the Roaring Twenties—or get overthrown by their own people, as happened in the 1860s when the fascist system that had taken over the Old South was destroyed by the Civil War.

But when oligarchies don't collapse or get overthrown, they morph into tyranny, and usually that happens within a single generation.

That's what happened in Russia. It went from the chaos of the 1990s oligarchy to Putin's authoritarian state in less than twenty years. It's also what happened in Hungary, where Viktor Orbán took a newly liberated democracy and turned it into an authoritarian state in less than a decade. It's also what's happening right now in Turkey, the Philippines, Brazil, India, and multiple other countries around the world.

Tyranny doesn't typically pop up all at once. It comes incrementally, moving step by inexorable step, until it hits a tipping point where it can no longer be stopped. Before that tipping point is reached, most people think the system will correct itself, that once everyone figures out what's happening, things will go back to normal.

They're almost always wrong.

America is now in that dangerous zone between oligarchy and tyranny. Our nation's oligarchs have controlled our politics for a solid forty years. They own the media, have captured the courts, and bought most of Congress. The question for today is whether they'll be satisfied with their comfortable oligarchy or whether they'll join Donald Trump's and the GOP's push for America's final transition to tyranny.

Steve Bannon told us what the goal was: "Deconstruct the administrative state." That's tyrant-speak for dismantling the institutions that might dare to—or have the power to—constrain oligarchic power.

As a result, we're in a race against time, and the window for successful action is narrowing. Every year that corporate constitutional rights remain in place, America's oligarchs tighten their grip. Every election they buy makes the next election easier to purchase. Every judge they install makes the next judge easier to intimidate or buy off.

This isn't alarmism: it's the historical pattern, repeated across dozens of countries and thousands of years. Oligarchies either fall or they become tyrannies; there's no third option.

In 2036, it will be 150 years since Davis wrote that corrupt *Santa Clara* headnote.

What will America look like?

Will we still be the world's richest democracy, and return to being a nation founded on the principle that "all men are created equal" and government should work first and foremost for We the People?

Or will we continue the Trump-blazed path of being a nation primarily serving a billionaire president, thirteen billionaires in his cabinet, billionaire media owners, and tech bro billionaires addicting our children to rage for their own profit?

The Dream That Was Stolen

In 1944, as millions of Americans fought fascism overseas, Franklin Roosevelt delivered one of his most important State of the Union addresses. He was too ill to travel to the Capitol building, so he spoke from the White House, his voice carried over this newfangled thing called radio into living rooms across America.

While he referenced the war effort in this speech, the man who'd rescued America from the Republican Great Depression leaned heavily on his proposal—what he called a Second Bill of Rights—to make America into what Jefferson called "a more perfect union." Its focus was a new set of constitutional rights that would guarantee the American Dream to *every* citizen.

"We have come to a clear realization of the fact," Roosevelt said, "that true individual freedom cannot exist without economic security and independence. Necessitous men are not free men. People who are hungry, people who are out of a job are the stuff of which dictatorships are made."

FDR's Second Bill of Rights laid out, as mentioned earlier, the rights to a job that pays well, small businesses to be free from unfair competition by monopolies, housing for all Americans, healthcare for all, and free college.

"All of these rights spell security," FDR said. "And after this war is won, we must be prepared to move forward, in the implementation of these rights, to new goals of human happiness and well-being."

FDR died shortly after that speech, on April 12, 1945, but over the next thirty-five years we came close to achieving that dream.

By 1980, two-thirds of Americans lived it. We had jobs that paid enough to support a family, we could afford to buy a home in our 20s, and healthcare didn't bankrupt us. We attended college without crushing debt, and for most of us, our retirement was secure. Ever since 1933, each generation had done better than the one before it.

Then Reagan was elected and—like Trump did with Project 2025—implemented the Heritage Foundation's 1,093-page 1980 "Mandate for Leadership," telling the oligarchs at the US Chamber of Commerce they should seize control of the media, the courts, America's universities, and public opinion.

While the Mandate's two thousand–plus recommendations didn't specifically cite Lewis Powell's infamous *Memo* or Davis's notorious headnote, it didn't have to: corporate constitutional rights were the obvious tool to accomplish most goals of the Foundation's billionaire founders and funders.

Reagan, the GOP, and the biggest businesses in America used corporate First Amendment rights to buy elections and drown out the voices of ordinary citizens. They used corporate property rights to battle every regulation that protected workers, consumers, and communities. They used corporate due process rights to block accountability for corporate crimes.

They crushed the unions that gave workers bargaining power, starting with Reagan's attack on the air traffic controllers' PATCO. They wrote the trade deals that would ship millions of good manufacturing jobs overseas. They turned healthcare and health insurance from servants of the middle class into raw profit centers. They transformed housing from a human need into a speculative commodity and loaded young people with debt for education that used to be free.

And they transferred over fifty trillion dollars from the homes and wallets and retirement accounts of working Americans to their own money bins.

FDR's Second Bill of Rights was never passed, but the dream it represented was real for the generations that watched and lived his expansion of democracy and an economy that increasingly worked for all.

But then Reagan and his "conservative" buddies used Davis's corporate constitutional rights headnote to kill even a hope for FDR's Second Bill of Rights.

Two Possible Futures

The two possible futures we face today aren't just about democracy or corporate power in the abstract. They represent starkly different visions of America: will we become more like FDR's ideal, or will we continue down today's road to oligarchic neo-feudalism like Russia and Hungary did?

Future One: Oligarchy Triumphant

In this possible future, the America of We the People fails. The billionaire oligarchs complete their capture of what's left of our democracy, corporate constitutional rights remain the law of the land, and wealth concentration accelerates until a handful of trillionaires own most of our politicians as well as everything else worth owning.

The middle class shrinks down to around 10 or 20 percent of us as the American economy comes to resemble the Victorian England that Charles Dickens wrote about in almost every one of his many books. Most Americans become permanent renters, never owning homes, never building wealth, and never achieving anything close to financial security. We work multiple jobs for oligarchs and corporations that face no democratic accountability, under conditions that grow steadily worse, for wages and benefits that somehow never keep pace with costs.

Healthcare remains unaffordable, education is financed by debt, and housing fully becomes a speculative playground for private equity and foreign investors. Climate change accelerates as fossil fuel corporations use their constitutional rights to block every attempt at regulation or the construction of alternative energy systems.

Democracy becomes nothing more than theater, like in most of the other oligarchies and tyrannies across the planet. Elections are held, but oligarchs fund all of the viable candidates and use their media and "free speech" to destroy any politicians who dare try challenge the system. The illusion of choice masks total corporate and billionaire control of our society and our governments, while the Constitution is twisted by a corrupt Supreme Court into a vestigial document that only protects their patrons and allies.

If this current trend continues and those of us who remember America before Reagan's corporate constitutional rights Revolution die out, the American Dream becomes a mere historical curiosity, a quaint, idealized past that young people skeptically read about in history books, a brief shining—but improbable—moment between the old aristocracies of Europe and the new oligarchies of the twenty-first century.

You could call it a new form of feudalism decorated with smartphones and compliant media, and it's where we're headed if we do nothing.

Future Two: Democracy Restored

In this future, democracy and the middle class win. The movement to end corporate constitutional rights reaches its tipping point and the Twenty-Eighth (or Twenty-Ninth) Amendment passes, explicitly stating that constitutional rights belong only to human beings.

With corporate constitutional rights stripped away, democracy can function again without corrupt Republican justices on the Supreme Court constantly constraining it. Congress is once again free to pass laws regulating corporate behavior without confronting endless constitutional litigation. States again revoke the charters of corporations that harm the public interest, corrupt executives once again go to prison, and local communities can again care for their people with revenues from taxing the morbidly rich.

Unions will recover and rebuild America as workers regain their bargaining power and union busting is outlawed. Wages rise to match productivity and the cost of living. And the fifty-plus trillion dollars that was stolen by the Reagan Revolution begins flowing back toward the working families whose labor created it in the first place.

Healthcare becomes a right like in every other advanced democracy in the world and ceases to be just another corporate profit center. Higher education becomes affordable again, and our public schools are rebuilt like Eisenhower did back in the day. Housing becomes a human need to be met, and exploiting it as a speculative commodity is outlawed or taxed into nonexistence. Climate change is addressed because fossil fuel corporations can no longer use their "free speech rights" to buy politicians and block regulation.

The American Dream is, in other words, reborn. Not the old dream of the 1950s, with its racial and gender exclusions and limitations, but a new dream for a new century. A dream where hard work is consistently rewarded, where every family can afford a home regardless of where or to whom they were born, where sickness doesn't bankrupt people, where education opens doors instead of creating debt prisons, and where each generation once again does better than the last.

This is the America we could bring about, and it all begins by exposing Davis's toxic headnote and using the public outrage to end corporate constitutional rights.

The Story They Could Tell

The newspapers and editorialists of the 2030s could write that in the 2020s people began to wake up.

They could chronicle how researchers dug through dusty law libraries and found the evidence of Davis's and Field's crime, revealed that the infamous headnote was a fraud and the oft-quoted *Santa Clara* decision never said what everyone thought it said. They could explain how, for 140 years, American democracy had been undermined by a lie, and the American Dream had been stolen by corporate oligarchs.

Activists organized. The Move to Amend Movement spread from community to community, educating millions. Towns such as Spokane, Lafayette, and hundreds of others passed ordinances rejecting corporate constitutional rights. States passed resolutions calling for a constitutional amendment.

The stories would document how the oligarchs fought back with everything they had, spending billions on propaganda while purchasing politicians, judges, and airtime. How they used every constitutional right they'd fraudulently acquired to prevent their own disempowerment.

But the people persisted.

Town by town, state by state, year by year, we educated neighbors. We ran for office, organized, and voted. We built a movement that finally broke through.

And in 2030, after decades of organizing, we passed the Twenty-Eighth Amendment to the United States Constitution, declaring that corporations are not persons and money is not speech.

As in 1865 in the South and 1933 nationwide, a third oligarchic era ended in America, and a new democratic age was kicked off. Corporate charters were revoked for corporations that harmed the public interest, monopolies were broken up, and wealth was redistributed through a return to rational individual and corporate taxation. Workers rebuilt unions, and communities regained control of their futures.

The American Dream, they'll write, was reborn.

It wasn't perfect. It wasn't quick. And it certainly wasn't easy. But it happened because ordinary people refused to accept rule by the morbidly rich—founded on the lie of corporate constitutional rights—as inevitable. Because we understood that the American Dream wasn't some nostalgic fantasy but a real achievement that had been stolen from us and our children, and we chose, instead of going along any more, to rise up and take it back.

Or the Story, If We Fail

Historians in the 2030s could also write a different story, explaining how in the early twenty-first century the climate catastrophe accelerated, killing millions and creating caravans of climate refugees. The billionaires and tech bro oligarchs tightened their grip on our lives and our news. As a result, what was left of our democracy after Trump's gilded presidency collapsed under the burden of corporate money and media manipulation. The American Dream became merely a bitter memory.

Some people, they'll tell us, saw what was happening. Researchers found the evidence of the 1886 fraud, activists tried to organize resistance, and a few communities even passed ordinances. A handful of states called for a constitutional amendment to reverse Davis's fraud.

But most Americans—struggling just to pay the rent and childcare bills—were too busy, too distracted, too exhausted, or too cynical to care. They knew the system was rigged; they just didn't believe they could change it, so they didn't even try.

As a result, the oligarchs won by default. Democracy died with a shrug, a footnote in a back section of the *New York Times*.

In this scenario, by 2050 America becomes a brutal, iron-fisted tyranny in fact as well as function. By 2075, even the pretense of democracy is abandoned to corrupt, strongman government based on the Russian and Hungarian system. The old US Constitution had become an anachronism, a museum piece from a bygone era when people naively believed in self-governance and dreamed of economic security for all.

The crime that started in 1886 and was kicked into high gear with the Reagan Revolution of the 1980s was never punished, the theft of constitutional rights never reversed, and the American Dream never restored.

The oligarchs won.

Climate collapse made much of the Earth uninhabitable. Billions died. Civilization fragmented. The survivors lived in a world of scarcity, surveillance, and oligarchic control. The historians of 2090, if any exist, would look back at the early twenty-first century as the last moment when change was possible, when people could have acted but failed to.

When the American Dream could have been saved but wasn't.

Which Story Gets Told?

America's future now depends on what you do.

Will you read this book and forget it? Or will you act?

Will you share this story? Will you join Move to Amend, Progressive Democrats of America, Public Citizen, or a similar organization dedicated to fighting corporate constitutional rights? Will you attend your local city council meetings and demand your community reject corporate constitutional rights? Will you organize your friends and neighbors? Will you vote for candidates who support the amendment? Will you run for office yourself?

Will you talk to your family about this over dinner? Will you explain it to your friends and acquaintances on social media? Will you help us make it impossible for people to plead ignorance?

Will you persist when it seems hopeless? Will you keep fighting when the oligarchs push back? Will you refuse to give up?

What you do today determines the history they'll write tomorrow.

A Final Word

Thomas Jefferson knew this day would come. In 1816, he wrote: "I hope we shall crush in its birth the aristocracy of our moneyed corporations, which dare already to challenge our government to a trial of strength and bid defiance to the laws of our country."

We didn't crush it in its birth but instead let it grow for two centuries. Now it's crushing us.

But it's not too late.

This bizarre, artificial aristocracy of moneyed corporations and their billionaire oligarchs can still be defeated. The morbidly rich can still be stopped, and democracy can still be reclaimed, restoring the American Dream.

The greatest legal crime in American history was committed in 1886. We're going to solve it.

We're going to restore the American Dream.

Join us.

Let us reclaim America's destiny, as Thomas Paine wrote in *Common*

Sense: "We have it in our power to begin the world over again. A situation, similar to the present, hath not happened since the days of Noah until now.... The reflection is awful, and in this point of view, how trifling, how ridiculous, do the little paltry cavilings of a few weak or interested men appear, when weighed against the business of a world."

WHO KILLED THE AMERICAN DREAM?

A Study Guide

Welcome and How to Use This Guide

Welcome to the investigation.

This guide is for readers, book clubs, classrooms, and community groups who want to go deeper into this story about how we got to the point where corporations have seized such enormous power in America. And it's really a true crime story, complete with a crime scene, a trigger-man, a mastermind, a cover-up worthy of Nixon, and a trail of victims stretching across more than a century.

You don't need to have attended law school to follow it, because the evidence has been sitting right there in plain sight ever since 1887 when the decision was published for the public. Use this guide in whatever way works best for your group: as a weekly framework, to jumpstart a discussion, or just an opportunity to get a few concerned Americans together to discuss our current crisis of democracy.

Chapter Summaries and Discussion Questions

Part I: The Crime Scene

Prologue and Chapters 1 and 2

Back in 2002, when my first book on this topic (*The Rise of Corporate Dominance and the Theft of Human Rights*) was published, I toured a few law schools to discuss it. I'd start out asking the students to raise their hands if they knew that in 1886 the Supreme Court ruled that "corporations are persons" with rights under the Bill of Rights and Fourteenth Amendment, and everybody's hand would go up—until I was done telling them this story.

Up until the past few decades, every law student in America was taught the same story about the 1886 Supreme Court case *Santa Clara County v. Southern Pacific Railroad*. They've been told the Court had ruled that corporations are persons under the Fourteenth Amendment. But the story isn't true. The actual decision, written by Justice Harlan, explicitly *refused* to rule on that question. It decided the case, instead, on a narrow technical matter about fence-post tax assessments and explicitly rejected the constitutional argument.

But as a headnote to that decision, in the case summary written by the Court's own reporter for publication in 1887, a single sentence appeared claiming the Court had decided corporations are constitutional persons. That sentence was *not* part of the ruling. It was *not* the Court's interpretation of the Constitution. And it was written by J.C. Bancroft Davis, a man with railroad stock in his portfolio and railroad oligarchs at his dinner table.

The Supreme Court arguments that preceded the decision pitted two very different visions of America against each other. One lawyer argued that the Fourteenth Amendment's guarantee of equal protection under law covered railroad corporations. The other argued it was written in the blood of the Civil War for freed slaves, not corporate officers and the companies themselves. Chief Justice Morrison Remick Waite interrupted the railroad's lawyer before he could even finish his argument that corporations should be considered "persons." The Court, he said, didn't need to hear it.

But then, a year later, the decision was published with a headnote saying that Waite had claimed corporations *are* persons. Something doesn't add up here: welcome to the crime scene.

QUESTIONS

1. When you first heard the claim that corporations were given constitutional rights, did it strike you as normal or strange? What does your experience tell you about how thoroughly this doctrine has transformed American business and political culture?

2. Why do you think no one seriously looked at the actual decision for over a hundred years? What does that say about the trust we so often place in official summaries like that headnote, versus original sources like reading the decision itself?

3. The railroad oligarchs of the 1880s controlled politicians, owned newspapers, and had a friend on the Supreme Court. Where and how do you see those same patterns playing out today?

Part II: The Suspects

Chapters 3 and 4

If this were a classic mystery novel, J.C. Bancroft Davis would be the guy who pulled the trigger. He wrote the fraudulent headnote, put words into the Court's mouth that the Court never said, and did it with a pen, not a gun. Nonetheless, the damage was very, very real and has transformed America and much of the rest of the world that imitated us.

Davis wasn't just some rogue clerk. He was Harvard educated, well traveled, a former diplomat, and briefly the president of his own regional railroad. His father had been the Governor of Massachusetts, and both had owned railroad stock. He moved in the same elite circles as the men who stood to gain enormously if corporations could claim constitutional protections against government oversight. You don't need a smoking gun when you've got motive, means, opportunity, and a letter he wrote to the Chief Justice himself asking whether his summary was accurate.

Chief Justice Waite's brief note back to Davis is one of the most revealing documents in American legal history. He told Davis the summary was probably close enough to what had been said before oral arguments (essentially confirming that corporations are artificial persons who can pay taxes and execute contracts), but then added that the Court had, in the actual decision, avoided ruling on the constitutional question of a broader personhood (like people have) entirely. He wrote that he'd leave it to Davis to decide whether to mention that the Court hadn't ruled on personhood in the official report. Davis decided not to, and by the time it was published, Waite was on his death bed.

Behind Davis stood the real mastermind of this crime: Justice Stephen J. Field. Field was a Gold Rush Californian who'd clawed his way up to the Supreme Court. He had a feudal worldview, was deeply in the pockets of the railroad oligarchs, and for the previous decade or more had worked on their behalf on the 9th Circuit Court of Appeals to get corporate constitutional rights under the Fourteenth Amendment established as law. Thus, for every case the railroads brought arguing for those rights (there were almost a dozen), Field was there in some capacity, nudging, dissenting against his skeptical peers, and building the intellectual scaffolding for this bizarre doctrine that the majority kept refusing to adopt.

When the majority chose not to reach the constitutional question in the *Santa Clara County* case, one of the final "California railroad tax cases," Field's strategy should have failed, but Davis made sure it didn't by spinning the decision in the headnote he wrote.

QUESTIONS

4. Davis likely never received a direct bribe; he just understood whose interests he served and acted on their behalf. Does that make what he did better or worse than outright corruption? Do you see similar patterns in politics or business today?

5. Field spent decades losing these cases before finally writing that headnote that flipped the *Santa Clara* decision on its head. What

does that kind of long-game ideological persistence tell us about how power really works in America?

6. The letter between Davis and Waite has been in the Library of Congress for over a century. Why do you think it took so long before a friend of mine found it when doing a search at my request?

Part III: The Long Set-Up

Chapters 5, 6, and 7

The crime of 1886 didn't just come out of nowhere. For seventy years before *Santa Clara*, corporations had been throwing case after case before the 9th Circuit Appeals Court trying to claim constitutional protections, and had lost every time. Field's colleagues on both the 9th Circuit and the Supreme Court kept saying the same thing: corporations are artificial legal entities created by government to serve public purposes, not human beings with inherent rights entitled to protection under the Fourteenth Amendment.

The oligarchs were battling the income tax, the direct election of senators, child labor laws, the eight-hour workday, antitrust enforcement, and pretty much every other reform that would later build what we came to call the American Dream. But they needed a constitutional weapon to stop all of it, and they couldn't win one honestly. So they turned to their buddies Justice Field and Court Clerk Davis.

The backstory goes further back than even 1816 when the Supreme Court first recognized corporations as "artificial persons" so they could pay taxes, execute contracts, and be sued in the *Dartmouth* case. The Founders and Framers didn't just fail to protect corporations in the Constitution; they deliberately kept corporations out of it altogether. They'd fought a bloody revolution against the British East India Company, then the world's biggest corporate monopoly, facing down the guns of the British Crown. They knew—and expressed their opinion loudly with the Boston Tea Party—exactly what unchecked corporate power looked like and wanted no part of it.

Thomas Jefferson warned about corporate power repeatedly. "Father of the Constitution" James Madison explicitly warned against it. The early states frequently revoked corporate charters—the "corporate death penalty"—when companies stepped out of line. That was the whole point: corporations were simply the creations of democratic government authorized by their charters, not autonomous entities with rights like the people who'd created them.

What happened between 1776 and 1886 isn't a mystery. Wealth concentrated, corporations grew, and ultimately the men who ran the railroads—then among the largest corporations in the world—had concluded that democracy was an obstacle to increasing their already swollen profits. They set about dismantling that obstacle one courtroom at a time, and when the courts kept saying no, they found another way.

QUESTIONS

7. Most Americans believe the Boston Tea Party was merely a protest against "taxation without representation." What changes when you understand it was actually a revolt against a corporate monopoly? How does that reframe your thoughts about where we are today?

8. The Founders were explicit that corporations should serve public purposes and could have their charters revoked if they didn't. Why is that idea considered radical today, and does it sound like common sense? What changed?

9. Corporations lost in court for seventy years before Field and Davis gave them their victory. What does that tell us about the relationship between democratic and oligarchic persistence?

Part IV: The Damage Done

Chapters 8, 17, and 18

The fraudulent headnote paid dividends to the railroad oligarchs almost immediately. Within three years, the Supreme Court itself was citing it as precedent without checking whether the original case had actually decided anything other than who should pay property taxes. By the end of the nineteenth century, the lie of corporate constitutional rights had become the law. And by the time Ronald Reagan took office in 1981, it had become a battering ram that politicians and courts would use to knock down much of what the Progressive Eras had built.

One of the quieter outrages of corporate constitutional rights is how the doctrine warped the basic rules of risk and accountability in business. Corporations could now claim First Amendment free speech rights to buy politicians, Fifth and Fourteenth Amendment due process rights to block regulations, and even Fourth Amendment privacy rights to keep, for example, the EPA from inspecting chemical manufacturing facilities. But when their factories poison a community's drinking water or their banks cause a financial collapse, their shareholders and officers are functionally shielded from liability. They get the same rights as we humans do, but without the accountability we'd face if we committed these offenses.

And there's the media. The consolidation of American news and entertainment, for example, into a handful of corporate hands wasn't an accident. It was enabled by corporations using their First Amendment "free speech" rights to buy politicians. As a result, media companies bought each other up, drowned out local voices, and turned the public square into a for-profit propaganda outlet. The result is an information environment where the oligarchs who benefit from the status quo pretty much exclusively own the megaphones that shape public opinion and decide both elections and policy.

Millennials today hold about 4.6 percent of the nation's wealth, but Boomers at the same age held 21.3 percent. That gap didn't come from laziness or bad choices by the last three generations. It came from the fifty-plus trillion dollars that the Reagan Revolution transferred, legally but fraudulently, from working Americans into the money bins of a handful of billionaires. Davis's headnote was the master key that made that possible.

QUESTIONS

10. If corporations get constitutional rights but still have limited liability, are they playing by the same rules as everyone else? What would

it look like to hold corporations genuinely accountable in the way real people, like you, are?

11. When you think about where you get your news and information, how many corporations stand between you and the original story? Does it change how you think about what you're reading or watching?

12. The gap in generational wealth between Boomers and later generations is enormous and growing. Did you see that as an individual problem before reading this book? Does the argument here change how you understand who's responsible for today's massive inequality?

Part V: The Verdict We Can Still Write

Chapters 12, 14, and the Epilogue

Here's the part that most "true crime" stories never get to: the part where the victims stand up and fight back.

This particular crime can be undone. A constitutional amendment—stating plainly that the universal human rights made explicit in the Bill of Rights and Fourteenth Amendment belong exclusively to natural persons, and not at all to artificial corporate entities—would do it. The activist group Move to Amend has already drafted the language. Twenty-seven amendments have already been passed, and now the job before us is to pass a twenty-eighth. Nothing less will really work in a permanent way (although legislation can take us a long way in that direction), because corporations will use those constitutional rights to litigate any lesser fix into the ground.

But the movement to reclaim human rights is already building, and has been growing for longer than most people realize. Starting in 2000, communities across the country began passing ordinances declaring that corporations aren't "persons" with constitutional rights within their borders. Rural Pennsylvania townships stood up against the companies drilling toxic injection wells. The city of Spokane took on corporate rights. Lafayette, Colorado, banned corporations from fracking. These weren't just symbolic efforts: they also worked as civics lessons, organizing tools, and the foundation of this larger movement.

The epilogue to this story isn't a comfortable one. We're in a race right now, and the window for action is narrowing as corporate and billionaire power continues to grow and threaten democracy itself. Every election bought by corporate money makes the next one easier for them to purchase. Each judge installed by oligarch- or corporate-funded campaigns makes corporate accountability harder to regain. The historical pattern—from Russia to Hungary to every other democracy that made the transition from democracy to oligarchy and then into tyranny—is clear enough: oligarchies either fall or they consolidate into something worse.

But the American Dream that was stolen using Davis's headnote is still within reach. FDR described it in 1944, and two generations came close to living it: jobs that pay a living wage, homes families can afford, healthcare that doesn't bankrupt us, education that opens doors to young people instead of saddling them with a lifetime of debt. That era prior to the Reagan Revolution wasn't a utopia; it was a functioning democracy for only about two thirds of Americans. But we built it once for white people and we can build it again for all Americans.

The question is whether we'll start before the window closes.

QUESTIONS

13. How have advocates for corporate constitutional rights deflected conversations away from their damage and corruption of our democracy, instead encouraging Americans to blame each other rather than corporations and oligarchs?

14. How has "culture war" served the interests of these corporations and the oligarchs they've created? What impact has this had on our political landscape and debates?

15. Do you think it's achievable to both pass a constitutional amendment through Congress and for the states to strip corporations of constitutional rights? What would it take to get us there, and what would need to happen first?

16. The communities that passed local anti-corporate-personhood ordinances knew courts would likely strike them down. Why do you

think they worked so hard to pass them anyway? What's the value of that kind of organizing, even when you can't win right away?

17. The book's epilogue lays out two possible futures. Which one feels more likely to you right now, and what would it take to change your answer?

Key Themes and Takeaways

1. This is an actual crime, not a mere metaphor. The *Santa Clara* headnote was a fraud that altered American history. A court reporter with personal conflicts of interest put words in the Supreme Court's mouth that the Court never said, and it became the legal foundation for everything that followed.

2. Corporate constitutional rights aren't just some inevitable aspect of capitalism. They're a specific historical invention, manufactured by specific people for specific reasons, which the Founders actively warned against and which courts rejected for generations before Field and Davis pulled off their crime.

3. The American Dream didn't just fade: it was defunded. The transfer of fifty-plus trillion dollars from working Americans to billionaires since the Reagan Revolution in 1981 was grounded in Supreme Court decisions based on Davis's headnote, and it gave corporations the legal weapons to block unions, fight taxes, buy elections, consolidate monopolies, and gut regulation.

4. The cover-up, therefore, was as important as the crime. For 140 years, lawyers, judges, and law schools simply didn't bother to check the original source. They cited Davis's headnote repeatedly in decisions starting in the late nineteenth century. That's how a well-placed lie became legal conventional wisdom.

5. History tells us what it takes to build and sustain a functioning middle class, as we did in the first half of the twentieth century. Two Progressive Eras built economies that genuinely served most Americans. We know the formula; we've done it before. The obstacle facing us isn't a lack of ideas; it's the set of constitutional weapons created

from Davis's headnote that we've allowed corporations to keep
pointed at what should be our democracy.

Action Ideas

Reading this book can be a form of activism, but it doesn't have to stop
there. Try one or more of these actions, alone or as a group, to spread the
good word.

† Learn about the group Move to Amend and their proposed Twenty-
Eighth Amendment. Share what you find with five people who
hadn't previously heard of it.

† Host a community teach-in using this book as the framework.
Davis's letter to Waite explicitly saying that they didn't consider the
constitutional question is a particularly powerful document to share
with people who haven't read the book.

† Research whether your city or county has ever passed any anti-
corporate-personhood ordinances. If not, kick-start that conversation with your local elected officials.

† Read *Democracy in Chains*, *The Shock Doctrine*, or *The Hidden History of the American Dream* to follow these threads deeper.

† Write letters to the editor, post on social media, and/or call your
representatives specifically about *Citizens United* and corporate
constitutional rights. Name Davis. Name Field. Make the history
concrete.

† Invite a local attorney, historian, journalist, or labor organizer to
talk with your group about how corporate constitutional rights show
up and make their work difficult.

"What Can I Do?"

Here are some prompts for individual reflection or group journaling after
reading this book.

† Now that I know where this started and who did it, what can I do to stop accepting its outcome as inevitable?

† What's one thing I'm willing to do, publicly, to help expose this fraud that's been hiding in plain sight for 140 years?

† Who in my life needs to know this story, and how can I tell it to them in a way that they'll understand?

There's no one right answer: only action.

Final Thoughts

This book started in a dusty Vermont law library with a photocopier and seventy cents' worth of change. It ended up being a story about who gets rights in America, who can consolidate wealth at others' expense, who gets heard in public, and who gets crushed.

The crime of granting corporate constitutional rights wasn't inevitable. The men who committed it made deliberate choices in service of their own wealthy class and that of their patrons. The fraud has survived to this day and has expanded through multiple Supreme Court decisions because enough powerful people found it convenient to let it stand.

But inconvenient truths have a way of eventually blowing up. The letter is in the Library of Congress. The decision itself (and Davis's headnote) starts on page 394 of the book published in 1887. Anyone can look.

Knowing about this crime against our democracy and our middle class is the first step toward undoing it. Now you know: what you do next is up to you.

The American Dream wasn't just lost. It was stolen.
And now we know who did it.

Notes

1. Howard Jay Graham, *Everyman's Constitution: Historical Essays on the Fourteenth Amendment, the "Conspiracy Theory," and American Constitutionalism* (Wisconsin State Historical Society, 1968). Contains one of the best detailed discussions on the "conspiracy theory" about Davis and Field [p vii].

2. Jeffrey D. Clements, *Corporations Are Not People: Reclaiming Democracy from Big Money and Global Corporations* (Berrett-Koehler, 2014) [p vii].

3. Details of the oligarchic takeover of America as mentioned here are covered extensively in my books *The Hidden History of American Oligarchy* (Berrett-Koehler, 2021) and *The Hidden History of the American Dream* (Berrett-Koehler, 2024).

4. *Munn v. Illinois*, 94 U.S. 113 (1876) https://supreme.justia.com/cases/federal/us/94/113/.

5. The taxation of property of railroad companies in California as affected by the Fourteenth Amendment of the Federal Constitution. Opinions of Justice Field and Judge Sawyer, delivered in the US Circuit court at San Francisco, September 17, 1883. https://babel.hathitrust.org/cgi/ssd?id=mdp.39015068206104;seq=11;num=3.

6. This is detailed extensively, with references, in my book *Unequal Protection: How Corporations Became "People" and How You Can Fight Back* (Berrett-Koehler, 2010).

7. Quoted from the headnote in *Santa Clara County v. Southern Pacific Railroad*, 118 U.S. 394 (1886) https://supreme.justia.com/cases/federal/us/118/394/.

8. Supreme Court, *Santa Clara County v. Southern Pacific Railroad*.

9. Supreme Court, *Santa Clara County v. Southern Pacific Railroad*.

10. Detailed at length in Hartmann, *American Dream*.

11. Ben Lefebvre, "Trump Pressed Oil Executives to Give $1 Billion for His Campaign, People in Industry Say," *Politico*, May 9, 2024, https://www.politico.com/news/2024/05/09/trump-asks-oil-executives-campaign-finance-00157131.

12. I document the progression of this through the Supreme Court via the *Buckley* and *Bellotti* decisions in the 1970s in my book *The Hidden History of the Supreme Court and the Betrayal of America* (Berrett-Koehler, 2019).

13. Hartmann, *Unequal Protection*.

14. Hartmann, *Unequal Protection*.

15. Hartmann, *Unequal Protection*.

16. Hartmann, *Unequal Protection*.

17. All of this is detailed in Hartmann, *Unequal Protection*.

18. Hartmann, *Unequal Protection*.

19. Detailed at length in Hartmann, *American Dream*.

20. Hartmann, *Unequal Protection*.

21. Hartmann, *Unequal Protection*.

22. Hartmann, *Unequal Protection*.

23. I document this at length in *The Betrayal of America*.

24. This is detailed extensively, with references, in my book *Unequal Protection*.

25. Detailed at length in *American Dream*.

26. Marilyn Geewax, "The Tipping Point: Most Americans No Longer Are Middle Class," NPR, Dec. 9, 2015, https://www.npr.org/sections/thetwo-way/2015/12/09/459087477/the-tipping-point-most-americans-no-longer-are-middle-class.

27. Ciara Torres-Spelliscy, "The History of Corporate Personhood," The Brennan Center for Justice, April 8, 2014, https://www.brennancenter.org/our-work/analysis-opinion/history-corporate-personhood.

28. *First Nat'l Bank of Boston v. Bellotti*, 435 U.S. 765 (1978) https://supreme.justia.com/cases/federal/us/435/765/.

29. https://www.opensecrets.org/news/reports/a-decade-under-citizens-united, More money, less transparency: A decade under *Citizens* published by Open Secrets written by Karl Evers-Hillstrom, with contributions from researchers Doug Weber, Anna Massoglia, Andrew Mayersohn, Grace Haley, Sarah Bryner and Alex Baumgart, Jan. 14, 2020.

30. Harriet Marsden, "Democrats vs. Republicans: Who Do the Billionaires Back?" *The Week*, April 8, 2014, https://theweek.com/politics/us-election-who-the-billionaires-are-backing.

31. Testing Theories of American Politics: Elites, Interest Groups, and Average Citizens. Published online by Cambridge University Press: 18 September 2014 https://www.cambridge.org/core/journals/perspectives-on-politics/article/abs/testing-theories-of-american-politics-elites-interest-groups-and-average-citizens/62327F513959D0A304D4893B382B992B.

32. Detailed at length in *American Dream*.

33. National Priorities Project, "2021 the United States Average Federal Income Taxes Paid." The average taxpayer in the United States paid $13,472 in federal income taxes in 2021. See where that money went, https://www.nationalpriorities.org/interactive-data/taxday/average/2021/us/receipt/ and Chris Edwards, "Corporate Welfare in the Federal Budget," CATO Institute corporate welfare tax analysis, stats for the year 2021, https://www.cato.org/policy-analysis/corporate-welfare-federal-budget-0.

34. Rick Perlstein, "Exclusive: Lee Atwater's Infamous 1981 Interview on the Southern Strategy," *The Nation*, Nov. 13, 2012, https://www.thenation.com/article/archive/exclusive-lee-atwaters-infamous-1981-interview-southern-strategy/.

35. Thom Hartmann, "A New War on the Vote," *The Progressive*, Feb. 11, 2020, https://progressive.org/latest/a-new-war-on-the-vote-hartmann-200211/.

36. Greg Palast, "Trump Lost: Voter Suppression Won," gregpalast.com, June 16, 2025, https://www.gregpalast.com/trump-lost-vote-suppression-won/.

37. Palast, "Trump Lost."

38. Democracy Now, "Ghost Wars: How Reagan Armed the Mujahadeen in Afghanistan," June 10, 2004, https://www.democracynow.org/2004/6/10/ghost_wars_how_reagan_armed_the.

39. A story about Mohammed Atta, the pilot of the first plane to crash into the World Trade Center, (author not specified), Biography.com, March 20, 2021, https://www.biography.com/crime/mohamed-atta.

40. CBS News report on Osama bin Laden being in Pakistan during 9/11, CBS News Staff, Jan. 28, 2002, https://www.cbsnews.com/news/hospital-worker-i-saw-osama/.

41. I cover this extensively in *The Hidden History of Big Brother in America.*

42. Move to Amend's summary of resolutions in support of a constitutional amendment, (undated), https://www.movetoamend.org/resolutions-in-support.

43. Move to Amend's President Greg Coleridge on the movement to abolish corporate personhood, *Corporate Crime Reporter,* Feb. 11, 2025, https://www.corporatecrimereporter.com/news/200/greg-coleridge-on-the-movement-to-abolish-corporate-personhood/.

44. (Author unknown), 2025 CPA-Zicklin Index of Corporate Political Disclosure and Accountability, Nov. 6, 2025, https://www.politicalaccountability.net/wp-content/uploads/2025/11/2025-CPA-Zicklin-Index.pdf.

45. Free Speech for People, State resolutions supporting a constitutional amendment, (undated), https://freespeechforpeople.org/state-resolutions-support-amending-constitution/.

46. "Billionaire Wealth Surges by $2 Trillion in 2024, Three Times Faster Than the Year Before, While the Number of People Living in Poverty Has Barely Changed Since 1990." Oxfam report predicts at least five trillionaires on the way, Jan. 20, 2025, https://www.oxfam.org.uk/media/press-releases/billionaire-wealth-surges-three-times-faster-in-2024-world-now-on-track-for-at-least-five-trillionaires-within-a-decade/.

47. Oxfam, "Billionaire Wealth."

48. Rachel Evans, Sabrina Willmer, Nick Baker, and Brandon Kochkodin, "With $20 Trillion Between Them, Blackrock and Vanguard Could Own Almost Everything by 2028," *Financial Post,* Dec. 4, 2017, https://financialpost.com/investing/a-20-trillion-blackrock-vanguard-duopoly-is-investings-future.

49. (Author unknown), "Wage Theft Costs American Workers as Much as $50 Billion a Year," Economic Policy Institute, Sept. 11, 2014, https://www.epi.org/press/wage-theft-costs-american-workers-50-billion/.

50. Hepworth, Gershbaum & Roth, PLLC, "Walmart Hit with $188 Million Verdict for Wage Theft Due to Lunch Break Violations," (undated), https://www.hgrlawyers.com/Articles/walmart-hit-with-wage-theft-verdict.html.

51. CDC data on tobacco use in the US, (undated), https://www.cdc.gov/tobacco/campaign/tips/resources/data/cigarette-smoking-in-united-states.html.

52. CDC data on opioid overdoses in the US, (undated), https://www.cdc.gov/overdose-prevention/about/ understanding-the-opioid-overdose-epidemic.html.

53. OSHA data on workplace stress and its deleterious effects, (undated), https://www.osha.gov/workplace-stress.

54. "Burden of Cigarette Use in the US," US News report on 100,000 Americans dying annually from corporate air pollution, April 4, 2019, https://www.usnews.com/news/national-news/articles/2019-04-08/100-000-americans-die-from-air-pollution-study-finds.

55. "The Lewis Powell Memo: A Corporate Blueprint to Dominate Democracy," Greenpeace published the Powell Memo in its entirety, Aug. 23, 1971, https://www.greenpeace.org/usa/democracy/the-lewis-powell-memo-a-corporate-blueprint-to-dominate-democracy/.

56. Judy Woodruff, "How Sinclair Broadcasting Puts a Partisan Tilt on Trusted Local News," PBS report on Sinclair Broadcasting and how they spin the news, Oct. 10, 2017, https://www.pbs.org/newshour/show/sinclair-broadcasting-puts-partisan-tilt-trusted-local-news 10/10/2017.

Index

The Last American President

A Broken Man, a Corrupt Party,
and a World on the Brink

Trump didn't break American democracy—he revealed how broken it already was.

In this urgent, deeply researched book, four-time Project Censored Award–winning, *New York Times* bestselling author Thom Hartmann argues that Trump is a symptom, not the disease. The real story is the ecosystem that built him: a childhood defined by cruelty, a mentor who weaponized shamelessness, a political party that sold its principles for power, and a donor class that used him to dismantle the guardrails on their own greed.

Inside, you'll find

- a psychological portrait of how Trump was made—not born;
- a clear-eyed account of how the Republican Party and billionaire networks enabled his rise;
- global comparisons to Hungary, Venezuela, and Weimar Germany—because this pattern has a name; and
- 7 proven, history-backed strategies for defeating authoritarianism before it becomes permanent.

This is not a book about despair. It is a book about recognition—and resistance.

The Hidden History Series

The Hidden History of Guns and the Second Amendment

The Hidden History of the Supreme Court and the Betrayal of America

The Hidden History of the War on Voting

The Hidden History of Monopolies

The Hidden History of American Oligarchy

The Hidden History of American Healthcare

The Hidden History of Big Brother in America

The Hidden History of Neoliberalism

The Hidden History of American Democracy

The Hidden History of the American Dream

Berrett-Koehler

Dear Reader,

Welcome to the Berrett-Koehler Community—a global network of changemakers creating positive impact in their lives, organizations, and communities.

Our Mission: Connecting People and Ideas to Create a World That Works for All

We believe transformation is possible. While outdated paradigms of self-interest, exclusion, and hierarchy continue to hold back our communities and organizations, we know that change can happen. That's why we connect people with actionable ideas from leading experts who are already creating the solutions we need.

The BK Way

We're an independent publisher that practices what we publish. Our books, digital resources, and community offerings provide practical pathways for building more just, equitable, and sustainable organizations and lives. Whether you're transforming your workplace, community, or personal practices, our publications meet you where you are with tools that work.

But we don't just talk about positive change—we live it. Through "The BK Way," we put stewardship and purpose before profit. As a benefit corporation, we're legally committed to benefiting all our stakeholders: authors, readers, employees, communities, and the environment.

As our gift to you, claim your free bestselling ebook at bkconnection.com/welcome. You'll also receive fresh leadership insights delivered to your inbox from bkconnection.com/blogs/the-bk-exchange.

You Make the Difference

We're grateful to our readers, authors, and community members, who bring our mission to life every day. Your stories of transformation inspire us and show others what's possible.

Share how BK publications are making a difference in your world at bkconnection.com/impact.

Your friends at Berrett-Koehler

Join the Berrett-Koehler Community

Are you passionate about supporting independent publishing and reading diverse voices and perspectives? Join the BK Community Membership Program and become a part of a vibrant literary community. To support mission-based publishing while saving up to 30 percent on all books and attending exclusive events, visit ideas .bkconnection.com/bkcommunity-join to learn more and become a member.